COPYRIGHT

CW01499986

FOREWORD

Elizabeth Alker

This is the story of my life, as I remember it, from an early age until the present time, October 2004. Hopefully, my autobiography will give my children, my grandchildren, and my great grandchildren insight into the life I had, as I, unfortunately, know next to nothing of my ancestor's lives and feel this is very sad.

I apologise to anyone it may offend, this is not my intention. These are the facts as I remember them, and I believe they are accurate.

THE ROAD FROM WIGAN PIER

Memories of a Lancashire Lass

ELIZABETH SMITH; CAROLE PARKES

ABOUT THIS BOOK

Carole Parkes

My years of family history research inspired me to encourage my mother, Elizabeth Smith, to write down her memories, so following generations may know about her life experiences. The words in this biography are mostly hers. I corrected them only when necessary to ease the grammar, make the meaning clearer, or to place events in chronological time periods. Bearing the above in mind, I edited the work and added references gleaned from my own studies.

As 2017 is the 80th anniversary of the year in which George Orwell's 'The Road to Wigan Pier' was published, I see this as an appropriate time to release this book. It shows one person's experience of living in close proximity to the area of Orwell's study in the same time frame he was there.

Hopefully, this account will also help others researching their family in the Lancashire area and further afield. Surnames included in this book are: ALKER, ASHCROFT, ATWELL, BARTON, BOOTH, BUTTERWORTH, CULSHAW, DAVIES, EDGAR, EVANS, FISHWICK, FOURACRE, HALLIWELL, HOLT, JOHNSON, RAWSTHORNE, PALMER, PENNINGTON, PHYTHIAN, REDDINGTON, SMITH, SPENCER, TABERNER, THISTLEWOOD, THULBOURNE, TURNER, and several more.

MY EARLY YEARS

I was born in Pemberton,[i] Lancashire, England, on the 24th February 1918, to very loving parents, James and Ellen Alker. A few weeks later, I was baptised in the church of St John with the name Elizabeth Alker. There was a difference of eighteen years between my parents, but the age gap never mattered, and I was brought up surrounded by love.

Both my parents came from big families, but we saw more of my mother's PENNINGTON side than we saw of my father's ALKER relatives. This was partly because we lived closer to them, but also because we were not favoured by my father's family. I will explain this more fully later.

My first memory must have been when I was about two years old. I can remember being pushed in an old fashioned push chair that was mostly made of wood. We lived in a very small house until I was about six years old. I believe it was number 4 Fairhurst Street. During the time we were there, I was very ill with croup. I remember mother having to bring the bed downstairs. She told me later I wasn't expected to live, but with love and care I pulled through.

I started school while we lived in Fairhurst Street, then we moved to a much larger house in the country. In fact, the house we moved to had been made into two dwellings at some time in the past. It belonged to my mother's uncle. His name was Isaac Barton.[ii]

"Down Brook," we used to say when asked where we lived; in fact it was Manor House Farm. I vaguely remember it was somewhere at the bottom of Brook Lane, near the Railway.

My mum's uncle and his family lived in the back of the house, and we occupied the front. Our dwelling had two lovely ground floor rooms, two bedrooms upstairs, and also a garret leading from one of the bedrooms. All the rooms were really large. I remember being a little afraid of the attic rooms because they were very dark. There was only one very small window. When my mother had to change the curtains, she would take me with her to show me there was nothing to be afraid of, but I was still frightened and would never dare venture up there on my own.

On one side of the house was a lovely orchard, and we had to cross a bridge over a narrow stream to get to it. This would have been Smithy Brook. Isaac's family, at that time, consisted of his wife, two daughters and a son. The boy, who was my mother's cousin, was also called Isaac. He used to tease me repeatedly, and would often tell me if I fell into the stream, a big fish would get me. I was terrified of falling in after that. Even so, it was a lovely place to live.

I was a lonely child. Often, I used to play shop on a very large boulder with stones or whatever else I could find. I did have one friend, a boy who lived nearby, but the poor boy was always ill. I spent a lot of time in his home keeping him company.

All this time, both my parents were working. My father, James Alker,[iii] was a labourer on his Cousin

John Alker's[iv] farm. It was called Chapel House Farm, and was sited at the end of Chapel Street. Father's pay was very low, so my mother worked in a cotton mill to help out. Father used to start work very early to feed the animals, then he'd come home in time for mother to go to work. He'd get me ready for school, give me my breakfast—which was mostly cheese and milk because I loved cheese and still do, and then he would take me to my grandparents' house until it was time for school. After he'd sorted me out he would then return to his work. I spent quite a lot of time at my grandparents' house when I was young. These were my mother's parents, William Pennington[v] and Elizabeth (nee Barton)[vi], and they lived in Brook Lane too. Their house was a small terraced home, no bathrooms or utility rooms in those days.

Mother was an excellent cook and used to go to night school for cookery. How we used to look forward to her coming home to see what she'd made. She loved giving parties and baking everything herself, and since our rooms were so big, it was no problem having people around. We had a lovely wide staircase and I used to love sliding down the banister rail. I have so many lovely memories of the years we lived there.

When I was about ten years old, we moved to a house only a few doors away from where my grandparents lived. I don't remember much about that house only that it was in Brook Lane, number 22. My grandparents lived at number 14, and when number 16, the house next door, became vacant, we moved there. It was much better in every way even though it was only a few doors away from where we lived before.

By this time, my mother had to give up work. She'd always suffered with her chest and working in a cotton mill hadn't helped at all. It was lovely being able to go home from school and find my mother there, and as an extra bonus I also had mother's family right next door.

My mother had two brothers and four sisters.[vii] Three of the sisters and the two brothers all still lived at home with my grandparents even though they were adults. Unfortunately, the two younger sisters couldn't work because they had tuberculosis, a disease very common in those days. The youngest, my Aunty Alice, was constantly in hospital. Nancy, the second youngest, was a lovely looking lady. She did work for a while but had to give it up. She made a lot of the family's dresses, and I used to follow her around like a lap dog because she was my favourite aunt. Another sister, Margaret Ann, worked in service and only came home now and again, so it was understandable why I loved Nancy so much, she was the one who was there the most.

None of these three sisters ever got married, but there was another sister who was already married. Her name was Anne and her husband's name was James Goulding. They had a son called William who was six months younger than me. We always called him Willie though and, like me, he spent a lot of his time with our grandparents in the house next door. Willie and I were the best of pals and did a lot of things together. We kept Chinchilla rabbits and fowl in our grandparents' yard. I also had a friend called Nelly Ashcroft and she also kept Chinchilla rabbits. My two uncles, William and John Pennington, who never married until much later when they were well into their thirties, made hutches for the rabbits and pens for the chickens.

Willie swore like a trooper, and despite our grandmother tipping off his mother about it, his mother didn't really believe it until she came round unexpectedly one day and caught him at it. Although I'm embarrassed to repeat it, Willie was naughty in other ways too. Once he had his back to me and I asked him what he was doing. Immediately, I'd wished I'd kept my big mouth shut for Willie was peeing, and as he spun around to show me, I got a mouthful of the horrid, wet stuff. I ran home screaming my head off. Still, despite this incident, Willie and I remained friends.

I had another male cousin, James Goulding. This cousin was several years younger than Willie and I. We often used to take him for a walk as we were very fond of him. All in all, we had a very good and happy life, but there were times when I did feel unbearably lonely. I remember asking my father why I didn't have a brother or sister.

His answer was always the same, "I love you so much, but if we have another baby in the house you'd get your nose pushed out."

He said he didn't want that, and I was satisfied with his explanation not knowing until much later the real reason. He'd been kicked by a horse on the farm at some point in his life and sadly couldn't father another baby.

SADNESS AND CHANGES

Two things happened in 1929 that upset our household very much. Firstly, my father, who had never been ill in his life, suddenly had to stay off work. The winter months had been very foggy and he'd been working out in all weathers. It was the black fog that caused his illness, and he was never able to work again. He did what he could to help out in the house instead. Unfortunately, this meant that both my parents were unable to work as my mum had already given up her job in the cotton mill because of her chest troubles.

The second event that upset the family was the death of my grandmother, Elizabeth Pennington, that year. She was fifty-nine and, unfortunately, was almost completely blind when she died. We didn't know it at the time, thankfully, but these events heralded a succession of tragedies that hit our close-knit family.

Just before I left school, things started to change for me too. There had been a new school built and I was lucky enough to go to it. It was quite different from the other schools I'd attended; it had far more space and a big gymnasium. Unfortunately, it made little difference to me as I only had twelve months to use it before it was time for me to leave school altogether. I was fourteen when I left.

A few years after my much loved grandmother died, I found a job in the same mill where my mother had worked. This was May Mills and was just over the fields from where we lived. At least, I was now bringing in some money. I soon realised that I wasn't too happy working there. I was so upset with the work; I found it difficult to eat my lunch. Every day my father brought me something fresh and tempting for lunch to try to get me to eat. He hated me working there too because he was worried the job would ruin my health as it had my mother's.

I was only there a few weeks before a friend of mine told me to go for an interview in the shirt factory where she was working. I got the job sure enough, but my wages dropped from one pound and five shillings a week, to just six shillings and sixpence. Less than half the money I was on at the mill. It was a huge drop in earnings but, nevertheless, my parents were pleased I no longer worked in the mill and, tellingly, they never complained about the lack of money to me. I enjoyed my work more in the clothing factory than I had in the mill. I was on a button machine and became very experienced at sewing buttons on accurately, except for one time I nearly sewed a button to my hand. I managed to pull my fingers free just before the automated action of the machine began.

One day a terrible thing happened. My father had been suffering from severe headaches for over two years and then, on the 22nd February 1933, two days before my fifteenth birthday, my beloved father died. After a terrible week of fits he'd had a stroke during the night and was paralysed down his left side. He was unable to speak that last morning, but the look in his eyes I shall never forget, even after all these years. His face had such a sorrowful expression, but he couldn't convey his thoughts to us.

It was worse for my mother than me because it meant she only had my small wage and a widow's pension coming in. The widow's ten shillings a week pension wasn't very much. To make ends meet, she began buying loose tea from Makinson's Arcade in Wigan. Mother carefully weighed it out, and then made it up into little bags she then sold. This wasn't very profitable though, so she gave this up and decided to take in lodgers. She quickly found a young married couple who wanted to live with us. The young chap was a miner and, after a while, we realised he used to beat up his young wife, Maggie. When they eventually got their own place, the Round House— so called because of its shape—she then took in a mother and son. After some time they also moved into a small house. Our home life carried on like this for some time with a succession of transient lodgers helping the family budget.

The August following my seventeenth birthday, a small fair came to our parish. There were about six or seven workmen who travelled around with the fair. These men needed a couple of meals a day, and a friend of my mother, who had taken these men in before, asked my mother if she could help her out and take three or four of the men. Of course, as we were between lodgers at the time, my mother was very pleased to help out. Each day, they came for dinner and tea. This lasted for just over a week until the fair eventually moved on.

Before they went, I got to know one of the lads. He was eighteen and very shy. His name was Walter Smith, a Liverpool lad, and I could tell he was only new to the job. Like many young girls, I would go around to the fair whenever I got the chance. On the Saturday, I saw Walter speaking to an older couple and, after a while, he came over to me and explained that the older couple were his parents, who had come up from Liverpool for the day to see him. He was wondering if my mother could give them a cup of tea before they returned home. I knew she would, of course, so I took them home with me. They stayed for a meal at my mother's insistence and in fact they all made very good friends.

Although the fair moved from place to place, our friendship with the Smith family grew stronger and eventually we met the rest of the family. They had two daughters, Hannah and Dorothy, and they also had another son, the eldest of the family. He was the last of the family to come and visit us.

Once I was out with Hannah and she said to me, "Do you like our Wally?"

Well the truth was I did like Walter, and I told her so. She then said, "Well if you like our Wally just wait 'til you see our George."

I didn't have to wait too long. Just a few weeks later, one Sunny afternoon, I saw these two cyclists who appeared to be lost because they were circling around. As they drew closer, I recognised one of them was Mr Smith[viii], Wally's father. I called them over and was then introduced to George, the eldest son. We were both very shy but immediately liked the look of each other. From then on we met as often as possible, but it was difficult as we lived twenty miles apart, he in

Liverpool and me in Pemberton. Little did I know then that he was to become my husband!

George used to come to our house for the weekend, and, on Wednesdays, mother and I would go to Liverpool to visit all the Smiths. Mother would travel early morning on the workmen's train then I would follow after I'd finished work. As time went on we started to stay the night in Liverpool, getting an early train home next morning so I could go straight to work. Neither George nor I had any money in those days. I was giving all my wages to my mother and she would give me back enough to cover my needs. If George and I went to the pictures it didn't matter which one of us paid, it would be whichever of us had any money at the time. Sometimes it was George and sometimes it would be me. George and his parents were in the same financial circumstances that my mother and I were in. His father was out of work and couldn't get a job. The 1930's were very depressing.

My mother always had a kind heart though, and so she asked the Smith family if they would like to come and live with us. She thought that perhaps Mr Smith would have a better chance of a job in our area. The Smiths were delighted. They knew that by sharing accommodation they could also share living expenses, and it would help my mother as well as them.

However, before the Smith family moved, George had a severe disagreement with his dad. At twenty-years-old, he'd received five shillings a week rise in his wages and hadn't told his father about it. His father, being out of work, was on the means test, which meant that everything coming into the house had to be reported. George had kept the money for himself because he wanted to take me out more, but it was wrong. It got his father into trouble with the Social Security people, as we call it now, because they sent him a letter. This letter was the cause of a blazing row between George and his dad, which resulted in his irate father telling him to go. Being just as angry himself, George packed his bags and left home. He went to stay with a friend from work until he could find somewhere else. This friend lived with his father. Sadly, his mother had died some years before so the domestic chores in that house were neglected. It wasn't ideal, but it was a place to lay his head.

The following Saturday, George didn't come down to see me. I was very upset because I didn't know something had happened between him and his father and was wondering why he hadn't turned up. The next morning I received a letter from him telling me all about the row and why he'd left home.

Of course, I was very upset and moped about the place until, in the end, my mother said, "Well, if you think that much of him, you'd better write and tell him." So I did.

George and I made arrangements to meet in a certain place in Liverpool. It was to be outside the Palladium picture house in West Derby Road. When I arrived, there was no sign of him there but, after a while, I spotted him on the other side of the road. He'd been watching me. He thought that I would think less of him because of the trouble he'd caused in the family.

Soon after this, his parents and two sisters came to live with us. Walter of course was travelling with the fair, and George was still not speaking to his father. The atmosphere was very unpleasant when George came down to our house to visit me and, sadly, this rift went on for a very long time.

I managed to get his sister, Hannah, into the shirt factory where I was working. We travelled together, walking there and back to Poolstock each day. It was at least a journey of two miles, and Hannah and I became real friends walking there and back like that. Mr Mann was the boss, and at fourteen-years-old I had thought this was a very silly name. I used to fall about laughing whenever I heard it, but it doesn't seem so daft now I'm older.

Mother had done a few alterations to the house to make it roomier. There was a front room called the parlour that we hadn't used when there was just the two of us. So she had a door installed in this room to lead to the big outside yard that had been repaved and given a face-lift. Mother had even had a new outside toilet installed at the bottom of the yard and a new boundary wall. The parlour could now be used as the new kitchen. The original one was quite pokey. Mother also went in for one of the first washing machines to come out. The lid had a handle that moved back and forth. We were very modern compared with granddad's house next door which still had an old midden in the back yard. All waste was emptied here and it was very smelly.

Meanwhile, things were beginning to get on top of George. He was working for a fruit merchant in

12

Liverpool, driving all day and doing a lot of heavy lifting at the end of his journey. He was still living at his friend's house in very bad, dirty conditions. Apart from the house never being clean it was also very cramped. So, being unsettled, George thought he'd try to find work nearer us.

By now, my mother's health was deteriorating badly. Every winter she suffered with severe bronchitis and each year it grew progressively worse. Although there was no doubt her employment in the cotton mills had caused her bad chest, there was no industrial compensation to fall back on in those days, as there is today. It was around about this time that her two brothers, who were living next door, found themselves girlfriends and got married. It had taken the death of my grandmother, Elizabeth Pennington, for my uncles to finally leave home.

Mother and I were still getting on well with the Smiths sharing our lives. Mr Smith had found work again, and they were beginning to get back on their feet with both him and his daughter, Hannah, having jobs. He had previously been an electrical wireman in Liverpool, but was now a factory watchman. Dorothy, the youngest of the family, was still attending school. Although the house was only small, we all managed quite well and I was pleased that my mother had some company of her own age. Mr and Mrs Smith and my mother often went out together when she was well enough, and the neighbours always jokingly referred to them as the three musketeers. They were happy days for the three of them, but it was destined not to last.

It all started with my Aunty Margaret. She was my mum's sister, the one I mentioned earlier who worked in service. Her job at Winstanley Hall[ix] was a live-in position so she was hardly ever at home, but one day she did come home feeling ill. It turned out to be meningitis and, eventually, the bed was brought downstairs in my grandfather's house to make it easier for my mum to nurse her. My lovely Aunt Nancy also helped, but it was too much for her, and she too had to take to her bed. Now, the only one left to look after both of them was my mother, and she wasn't in the best of health owing to her chest complaint. My old granddad did all he could to help, of course, but he was old and feeble himself. Although it's sad to say this, it was a blessing for my mother that her younger sister, my Aunty Alice, was in hospital again during this time. Otherwise, there would have been three sick patients for her to look after.

Within a week of taking to her bed, my beloved Aunty Nancy died. They held her funeral back because they had no hopes of Aunty Maggie recovering from the meningitis either and, sure enough, a few days later, she died too. We had a double funeral for them. I can still picture them now lying in granddad's front room. Nancy looking so peaceful as if she were merely asleep and poor Margaret with much suffering etched into her face.

Shortly after this sad event, I had my eighteenth birthday and realised soon after it I was in trouble. Sure enough, even though I hadn't been to the doctor, I knew I was pregnant. In a way, it was the best thing that could have happened for George, living as he was in that dirty house in Liverpool with his workmate, yet having to tell the family was a worry. We faced them together. Mother wasn't too upset when she realised that George wanted to marry me straight away. She was rather pleased in a way, because she knew her own health was deteriorating and she was worried what would happen to me, her only child, if I was left all alone.

Our marriage, just three months after my eighteenth birthday, was a quiet affair really with mother as usual seeing to everything in her quiet, efficient way. Despite the rush, she even made a lovely cake. The only thing that marred our day was the fact that George's father, William Smith, who was still not speaking to George, refused to attend the wedding. We later found out that he did come to the church and watched us from a distance.

My granddad, William Pennington, now lived alone in the house next door while we still had the Smith family living with us. It was quite cramped. Although granddad's daughter, Alice, was still living, she now remained permanently in hospital, only coming home on very rare occasions. Since granddad was effectively on his own and needing more than a little care himself these days, we all decided it would be best if mother, George, and I all went to live with him in his house, thus leaving our house and all its furnishings free for the Smith family. This arrangement worked out very well.

Life settled down for a little while. The only thing that blighted our life was that George still had to travel to Liverpool to work every day. He was still working in the fruit trade because he'd been unable to find work nearby as planned. It was 1936, about the time George Orwell was in Wigan writing his book 'Road to Wigan Pier'. Tuesdays and Thursdays were particularly troublesome since he had to be at the Liverpool market by five thirty on those mornings. So George made arrangements to stay overnight in Liverpool with his paternal grandmother and his aunt on Monday and Wednesday evenings. His paternal grandmother's name was Mary Jane Smith, but before she married her surname was Holt[x]. This made his working life a little more manageable, especially since I used to help him by getting up very early on the mornings he was in Liverpool and going off to buy his workman's return rail ticket. I used to mail it to him at his grandmother's address and he always received it the same morning I sent it, it was never once late. The post was extremely reliable back then.

Just ten minutes before midnight, one cold winter night in 1936, we had our first baby—a boy. He was lovely. My mother saw to everything again. I had him at home in my granddad's house and we called him Brian. I will always remember his birth; it was so lovely. Later, I was told that my granddad, William Pennington, was kneeling by his old rocking chair praying for me the whole time. George came home from work that evening and my mother had to send him straight back out again to fetch the doctor. In February 1937, just a couple of months after Brian's birth, my granddad died. This left my mother, George, the baby, and me in the house.

After granddad's funeral, life settled down once more for a short while until George mentioned again that he was growing tired of all the travelling. It was also expensive. In the end, we both knew we couldn't carry on like that, so we decided to do something about it.

One day, I went to Liverpool with George's father. He knew one of his old neighbours in 22 Palatine Street would be able to help. This was Mrs Lennon who was also a relative, and good enough, she knew a lady in the next street who lived on her own in a large house. It seemed probable that this lady would take in lodgers so we went around to 11 Woodbine Grove to see her. This lady took pity on us and decided to rent off some rooms to us.

Back home again, I began to work out our expenses with my mother and mother-in laws' help. After sorting this out, we then worked out how much money we'd have left over for furniture. This done, the three of us set off to buy some essential furniture to start us off. Now I don't know who to blame for this, mother, mother-in-law or myself, but we ended up buying far more than we'd originally intended. We purchased a lovely sideboard, three piece suite, two carpets and a sweeper. Altogether it cost fifty pound, quite a lot of money in those days. When George came home from work and I told him how much I'd bought on credit he nearly had a fit. George being George, he soon recovered and forgave me.

So in due course we moved to Liverpool. Mother had arranged to move back in with the Smiths once we'd gone so she would have some company.

17

Our two rented rooms at Woodbine Grove looked lovely with the new carpets and furniture. I soon got into a routine with my housework as most women do. Leading up to the front door was a long garden path and two steps. Every Friday I used to sandstone all the way down from the front door to the garden gate. It looked beautifully white when I'd finished. Unfortunately, apart from our two rooms, one upstairs and one downstairs, the rest of the house was mostly uncared for. May, the woman who we shared with, was out most of the time so didn't seem to bother with much housework. In the end, we used to laugh about it because instead of changing her bedding she used to change beds. She had two bedrooms, and when the bed became too soiled to sleep in it anymore, she would just go into the other bed for a few weeks until that too became grubby. Then, of course, she would have to do something about it, but washdays for May were very few and far between.

I used to go and see my mother as often as I could, and she would spend a day or two with us. Despite me repeatedly asking her to come and live with us in Liverpool, she was reluctant to do this because she feared her chest would be worse in the smoky city. Besides she was quite settled with the Smith family.

Just before Christmas 1937, when Brian, our baby, had his first birthday, we received a parcel from my mother. I remember eagerly opening it. Inside was a little pink dress and a matching coat, more suitable for a little girl than a boy, but it was lovely. In those days, little boys were often put in dresses until they were a bit older so it didn't matter too much.

As usual in winter, mother started with a bad attack of bronchitis again. By the time my twentieth birthday came around in February 1938, I received a telegram from my father-in-law to say my mother was very ill. So, of course, I began travelling back and forth from Liverpool to Pemberton with the baby.

After only a few days of this, I was in Liverpool doing some shopping before making the journey up there when my father-in-law and Walter came looking for me. As soon as I saw them, I knew from their expressions what they had to tell me. My dear mother was dead. I went back to the hospital with them to identify her. She was only forty five years old, but it eased my pain a little to know she was now with my beloved father. In my heart, I knew she'd never really been happy since he died. Over the past five years since his death, she'd often said that she wished she could be with him, and I knew it was only the thought that I was so young that had kept her going. The fact I was an only child worried her, especially knowing she was in ill health. Once she'd seen me married and settled, she was happier. She knew George would look after me.

Mother always thought a lot of my husband and his family and George well deserved her praise. For the next twelve months I did nothing but cry. In just a few short years, from when I was fourteen to twenty, I'd lost my grandmother, my father, my two beloved aunts, Nancy and Margaret, my granddad, and now my mother. It was just too much to bear. I felt there was no-one left for me except, of course, George, who was my rock. With his support, the pain did finally ease.

I often wonder how I would have fared if I hadn't been married, but God works in mysterious ways, and even though I was a sometimes lonely, only child, I've certainly got a lovely family around me now. That will be written about later though.

EARLY WAR YEARS

For the next eighteen months or so, we got on with our lives as best we could. George and I never had much money, but we always managed to keep our heads above water and we were reasonably happy.

In April 1939, my husband joined the Territorial Army. The friend he'd gone to stay with, after that row with his dad, had already joined up, and he'd been discussing with George the benefits of being in it, like the extra money and going off to camp. Of course, my husband thought it was an excellent way of earning a little bit more. If only we'd known then that war was just around the corner, I don't think he'd have been so quick to join up.

One day, soon after he'd joined, I heard a knock on our front door. I opened it and found a stranger standing there, a young lady about my age. She told me she was Hugh's wife. Hugh Davies was my husband's friend from the Territorial Army, so I naturally invited her in. Her name was Peggy, and she'd come to ask George to pass a message on for her husband. Hugh was unable to attend the Territorial Army meeting that night as he'd been taken to hospital with appendicitis. That was the start of a very long friendship with Peggy.

On the 3rd September 1939, only five months after George had joined the Territorial, we received a telegram calling my husband up for the regular army. George was at work so I went to his firm, at the top of our street, to find him. He wasn't there as he was out in the lorry delivering vegetables. His boss phoned around for him though, and he came straight away because he had to report immediately to Headquarters. Now, after all the loss in my short life and with me only twenty-one and Brian not yet three, my husband was off to fight a war, perhaps never to return. I was devastated. Peggy and I both went to the barracks to see our husbands off. Then from there, even though it was late in the day, she kindly asked me if I would go with her to see her mother who lived in Dingle. She knew I had no family to turn to so it was very kind of her to invite me. I would have felt lost on my own.

We caught a tram, there were no buses then, and that same night they were going to have a trial blackout. We were travelling on top of the bus and just as the conductor came around for our fare; all the street lights went out for the blackout. Naturally, all the bus lights were off too and in the confusion I dropped my few coppers fare. Peggy and I were in tucks laughing and we were crying too. The unexpected hilarity of that scene had unleashed all the tensions we were feeling, knowing our husbands were preparing for war. Anyway, as it was only a trial thing the lights came back on again quickly and we managed to sort out the fare. It gave us a taste of what was to come though.

When we got back to my house, Peggy decided to stay the night. Neither of us wanted to be on our own just yet. We felt we needed companionship with our husbands away. Going into the darkened house and switching on the light we were surprised to see George sitting by the window in the dark. Of course we wanted to know why he was home and Peggy was all excited thinking if George was here then Hugh must be waiting for her too. George had no idea if Hugh was home or not, all he knew was that he himself had missed the last train to Chester where he was supposed to be reporting for duty. He'd have to go first thing in the morning instead. George took Peggy home and she was very disappointed that Hugh wasn't there. At least, George and I did get one more night together before he left again.

Peggy and I spent a lot of time together during those first months when our husbands were both away. Every Sunday we'd dress up and go to visit one of George's aunties who also lived in Liverpool. This was his Aunty Lily, his dad's youngest sister. Her name was Rose Lily[xi] but everyone just called her Lily. Brian had a lovely duffle coat and a pair of leather gloves. He looked quite a little toff. Peggy had no children so it was just the three of us. She and I both had good coats, and we each had a lovely hat that was all the fashion in those days. It was the same every week, and we always ended up having a really good laugh because before leaving the house, we would ask each other how much money we had.

Peggy would say, "Tuppence".

That would be about the same as I had, not very much at all. So then we had to decide whether to walk there or walk back. We couldn't afford to take the tram both ways. We were both young and healthy though so we really didn't mind walking at all.[xii]

Peggy stayed overnight with me for much of the time our husbands were away. The raids would start about seven thirty in the evening and although there were air raid shelters outside we didn't use them, mainly because people screamed and cried in them, and we found it very unsettling. If Peggy hadn't stayed with me, I would have been in that big house on my own for most of the time because May, the lady we shared with, was never there. Every morning about half past nine she'd go to Mass. I don't know what she did for the rest of the day, but she'd come home about four o'clock in the afternoon and then get ready for work. She worked in a theatre starting about half past five. Most nights she couldn't get home from work because of the air raids, but I remember one particular night when she did manage to make it home.

Usually when the sirens went, Peggy and I used to come downstairs with Brian and go into my sitting room. This was the only room in the house with heavy, wooden shutters fitted to the windows on the inside of the house and we felt safer there. At least we were protected from flying window glass. On this particular night, May was in the room first and being unused to my furniture arrangement she fell over something in the semi-dark. Peggy and I could do nothing but laugh. Fortunately, May was laughing too, so it was alright.

Although there were many times when I was on my own with Brian, I never remember being afraid. Later, on one of his army leaves, George reinforced the cupboard under the stairs so it was very strong under there. This must have been after the home office advice that underneath the stairs was the safest place in a house. From then on whenever we heard the sirens, we'd take the cushions off the suite and place them on the floor in the cupboard.

Brian would then say, "Put my coat on mummy and let's go under the stairs."

He was a darling, so brave for just a young child and, I suppose, I drew strength from him. I prayed a lot under those stairs but, the funny thing was, I never prayed for us, only for my dear husband. I used to write to George every day and he wrote to me whenever he could. There were times, however, when things were very difficult for him and then he couldn't write home. I don't know how, but somehow I knew George would come back safely. Even though the radio news was sometimes very worrying, I never lost that faith. I used to detach myself from the bad news, somehow, so that I never felt part of it.

By the time we heard the radio broadcast about Dunkirk, Peggy's visits were less frequent. Although we'd depended on each other for mutual support at the beginning of the war by this time our friendship was beginning to disintegrate. I think this was mainly because she'd suffered a miscarriage and felt the need of her mother more.

Fortunately, although they'd had a really tough time at Dunkirk, both George and Hugh made it home safely from there. It was a terrible time as everyone knows and I could only imagine the way it was whenever George tried to tell me about it. He'd seen many of his comrades killed right beside him. The men returned to England with nothing, having to train and build up their troops again.

George was a driving instructor and after a while was made a Bombardier. In 1940 my husband's regiment, the Kings 59th Mediums; Field Regiment and Royal Artillery, moved to Dunwich on the east coast. In one of his letters he asked if I would go down there for one month because he was due some leave in December. I decided to go and waited for a letter to say he'd found us somewhere to stay. In the meantime, I remember buying some wool and making myself a navy blue skirt and cardigan, and also a pale green jumper to complete the outfit. I knitted all these in a month because I wanted to look smart for George whom I hadn't seen for a long time.

I went down by train early in November; it was a long journey with Brian. When we finally arrived in Dunwich, George was waiting for us with an army lorry. We had to jump in quick for he really shouldn't have been there. It was a good job we were well wrapped up because it was bitterly cold—Dunwich was right on the coast. George drove us to a beautiful country cottage that was owned by a Miss Palmer. She was a retired midwife, a very nice person but extremely strict. After introducing me, George had to quickly return to his duties, and Brian and I were then left alone with Miss Palmer.

We got along very well until teatime. Brian was eating his food with a spoon but our new landlady thought he should be using a knife and fork. I was very touchy in those days, well I suppose I still am, and taking her criticism to heart I became upset and was soon in tears. That's when George came back. He was, of course, surprised and a little concerned to find me crying. I suppose Miss Palmer was too. We soon became accustomed to each other's ways though, and in the end we got on quite well. I was much younger than she was and, therefore, could easily adapt to her pattern of living. She was very set in her ways. Everything had to be just so. Even the tablecloth had to be folded in exactly the same folds I found it in before I put it back in the drawer. Woe betide me if I folded it differently. I took great care to put things back exactly as I found them, and owing to my thoroughness, we soon got on like a house on fire.

Every afternoon Brian and I would take a walk through the small village then cross over to the other side of the road where we could enter the woods. It was a very cold winter that year, and on our trips we would gather lots of fir cones for the fire, which always pleased Miss Palmer.

George came to visit often, as soon as he'd finished his daily duties. Then, one day, he came to tell me he was moving on with the regiment. He was only going to Leiston, a nearby village, but he wanted us to move with him. He left on the Friday and said he'd come back for me on the Sunday. This he did. On the Sunday I was watching out for him coming along the path. When I spotted him I ran inside the house to tell Miss Palmer and to collect my bags. We'd made such good friends by then that Miss Palmer and I were both crying as George and I left her.

Once again George had borrowed a lorry and we drove to the home of a Mrs Atwell. Strange how well I still remember all the names and faces of these people from the past. Mrs Atwell was also on her own, a widow who was used to taking people in. She had a four bedroom house but we had to pass through her bedroom before reaching ours. As usual, George had been given a sleeping out pass, so Mrs Atwell fixed up some kind of cot for Brian and George slept with me.

Leiston was a much larger place than Dunwich, almost a small town in fact. I was pleased about that because now I had a multitude of shops to browse around. One night we even went to the pictures, but I remember the film breaking down and they were unable to fix it. To compensate, we were given free tickets to go again the following Friday night. George and I decided to buy an extra ticket for Mrs Atwell since she had been so helpful to us with the cot. She could then come along too.

On that first Friday morning I came downstairs and went into the front room. Spotting a bill on the table and thinking it was probably mine for the accommodation, I examined it more closely. I was right; it was our bill and what I saw nearly frightened the life out of me. Every tiny thing was listed, so much for the cot; so much for George staying the night; every meal and lots of other less obvious services were all written down and charged for. We certainly didn't expect to stay there for nothing, but this account was for far more than George and I were getting even though as a Bombardier he'd been given a small wage increase. We hadn't even been there a full week yet as we'd only arrived on the Sunday. I was so annoyed.

I anxiously waited for George to come in and, being winter, he arrived in his heavy, army coat. When I told him about the bill, he didn't bother taking his coat off;

he just waited for Mrs Atwell to come back. When she came in, George asked her for the bill and, sure enough, it had been our bill on the table. I can't remember now all that was said, but we ended up giving her every penny we had between us. That left us with absolutely no money at all until the following Tuesday, payday. We still went to the pictures that night on the free tickets we'd been given, but I'm afraid we didn't take our friend as intended. We obtained a refund on that ticket instead.

With only a week to go before George was due his leave and could return home, we had to find somewhere quickly just until we could leave. One of George's friends had his wife staying in Leiston, and they came with us to help us find somewhere. The four of us split up and were knocking on doors individually. Brian, of course, was with me. None of us were having any luck until George and I knocked on a few doors together. By this time we'd almost given up. However, the next door we tried, the daughter of the house thought they might be able to help.

She asked us in while she explained to her parents what we needed. Her mother was very old and badly afflicted with arthritis, yet they kindly offered to put us up. George was able to stay too as he had his sleeping out pass.

The week passed pleasantly and quickly. I tried to help as much as I could in the house and in particular, they had a lot of brassware that I paid special attention to. I must have been a good help, because they asked us to go back and stay with them again after George's leave was over. When we asked for the bill here, they wouldn't take a penny from us. They were so kind, so different from Mrs Atwell who obviously made a very profitable living from taking people in.

It was good to get back to Liverpool to our own home and be a little family again, but it didn't last long. George was soon on his way back to join the regiment again. It felt strange to be alone once more with just Brian for company. Poor love, he couldn't understand why his daddy had gone away yet again. Meanwhile, the raids in Liverpool were growing worse and we had to go into our own shelter more often.

Being away so often meant we'd not been in contact with George's parents for a while. I hadn't given it much thought really. We were all so busy with our own little day-to-day problems that we forgot just how much they worried. Despite the ongoing rift between George and his dad, they were still eager for our news. My father-in-law was working in war work by this time, and when I did eventually go and visit them, I noticed how much better off they seemed to be. I was pleased about this because Mr Smith had turned into a very bitter man during his years of unemployment, and it had been bad for them all. It was during this time of heavy bombing that George's brother, Walter, came to see me with his new wife. They'd married at the beginning of the war when I was in Dunwich.

Walter had only been in the forces for a short time. He'd been a physical training instructor and was very fit, but suddenly something went wrong, and after a medical he was invalided out of the army. His wife, Gladys and her mother had a small general shop, and so when Walter came out of the army he joined them in the running of it. He hoped to make it more successful. They'd just opened a second shop before their visit to me. They had come to invite me to stay with them for a few weeks, so Brian and I could get away from the bombing and get some decent sleep. What a joke that turned out to be! We had many a laugh over this for, as it turned out, they lived near a Chemical factory. This was the I.C.I.[xiii] plant in Runcorn. They couldn't have been in a more dangerous spot themselves. I spent two weeks with them but, to be perfectly honest, I would have had a more peaceful time at home.

A short walk from their house was the railway, and it ran alongside three caves made out of rocks. How they came to be there in the first place I didn't know, unless they were from the First World War. These caves had iron trestles in them and people would take bedding and sleep on them during the air raids. Everyone seemed to have their own place and so did we. We would go there about half past five every afternoon and come back about six o'clock in the morning. It's amazing what discomfort you can put up with in an emergency. On our arrival back at Walter's house, Brian and I were always told to go to bed for an hour or two, but my sister-in-law and her mother would get ready to open the shop. Despite the nightly excursions to the caves, Brian and I did stay with Walter and Gladys for the full two weeks before we caught the train back to our home in Liverpool.

Arriving back at Edge Street station, we were faced with a long walk home via Kensington, and then on to Boaler Street and eventually home. It was tiring enough with a suitcase and a little boy in tow but, as if this wasn't enough to contend with, just as we got to Boaler Street, the sirens went and I heard the plane as it came directly overhead. On top of everything else it had begun raining. I dived to the wet floor as quickly as I was able, pulling Brian with me, just as we'd been instructed to do if caught in this situation. There was a shelter nearby but I didn't dare risk going there, so we stayed were we were, and I protected Brian as best as I could with my own body while holding my breath.

Eventually, the planes passed over and once the sound of their engines subsided, we dashed to the shelter. There was a young girl inside with her boyfriend and she was screaming. He tried to quieten her down but to no avail. Once the 'all clear' sounded, Brian and I left the shelter and headed for home again.

The bombing caused a lot of damage in Liverpool that night. From our own little shelter under the stairs, we could hear the planes droning over, and we heard several bombs explode. It was very frightening. When we awoke next morning, we didn't know what we'd find. We heard later that a bomb had dropped on a school killing several hundred people, and that was quite near to the spot in Boaler Street where Brian and I had lain on the floor.

In November 1940, George was moved to Histon, in Cambridge. We were still writing to each other every day at that time, and after a few weeks of settling in, George asked me if I would join him there. My husband and two of his friends went looking for lodgings on a large housing estate. They were all hoping to bring their wives there. They were successful, and the two other wives and I all travelled to Cambridge after Christmas.

I can't recall how many children the other wives had but I know I was the only one with just one child.

Arriving in Cambridge station, we were hoping to find our men folk waiting for us. George was nowhere to be seen but the other two husbands were there, and they informed me that George was ill in hospital. I was very upset and worried, but George's friends took us to the lodging they had found for us. We were all to be staying quite near to each other, which was a blessing because it made me feel a little less vulnerable. Mrs Thulbourne, my new landlady, made Brian and I feel very welcome. She knew all about George being in hospital and promised to take me there the following day. It was growing dark by this time and, after we'd eaten, Brian showed signs of wanting to go to bed.

The next day was a Sunday, and Mrs Thulbourne kept her word and took us to Addenbrook Hospital in Cambridge. George was lying flat on his back on a bed placed out on the veranda. He looked so ill, but then that was understandable as he'd not eaten anything for days. He was only being allowed milk because they'd discovered he had a perforated stomach ulcer. In time, he recovered enough to leave hospital and start his convalescence. While he was regaining his health he came regularly to see me at Mrs Thulbourne's home and she, being such a kindly soul, couldn't do enough for him. Everything was rationed, and despite the fact she'd queued half the morning for it, she would give up her fish so George could have it. Thanks to her generosity George was soon well enough to return to his unit. We now believe his ulcer could have been caused by his experiences on the beaches at Dunkirk.

At that time, food was so scarce he'd pick up anything that looked remotely edible and eat it.

Once he was back with his unit, George moved with the regiment to Yorkshire. Mrs Thulbourne had become such a good friend that Brian and I stayed down in Cambridge with her. George travelled miles to come and see us there, more often than not, walking alongside the railway lines when he couldn't thumb a lift. Brian would have been about four years old at this time. The two women I'd travelled down with had long since returned home, but I liked living in Cambridge and was happy to stay. With no close family of my own, it was an easy decision.

Mr Thulbourne had been shell shocked during the First World War, and so I had to take Brian out for most of the day in case he was too boisterous and annoyed him. I probably worried needlessly though, because Mr Thulbourne did seem to enjoy Brian's company, often taking him down to his allotment for the day.

The Thulbourne's seventeen year old son worked in Chivers, making jam. One day Mrs Thulbourne approached me and asked if I'd like to enrol Brian in school and maybe try to get a job in Chivers myself. I thought it an excellent idea if she didn't mind collecting Brian from school for me and seeing to him until I returned from work. She was willing to do this so, in a very short time, Brian was settled in school and I was in Chivers employment. Now I was really getting on my feet financially. George's army pay was slowly increasing, and I was bringing in a wage. On top of this,

I was also in receipt of two pounds a month from my Uncle Sam.

I haven't mentioned my Uncle Sam before because he's on my father's side of the family and, as I said at the beginning, I had more to do with my mother's family than my father's. Now I've brought him up, it's a good time to tell you all I can remember about my father's family. Their surname was Alker. From all I can remember, they were mostly farmers or had an occupation to do with the land, like wheelwright or blacksmith.

Apart from spending a few holidays with them when I was quite young, I never really had much to do with them. My grandfather[xiv] on my dad's side had Melling's Farm, in Winstanley. His father, my great grandfather,[xv] was also a farmer. Several generations of Alker farmers have worked the land in Lancashire, way back to the 1600s at least.

MY FATHER'S FAMILY

My father, James Alker, was brought up on the farm he was born in. This was Mellings Farm in Pemberton, or so it says on my dad's birth certificate. We always thought it was actually in Winstanley, anyway, no matter. The boundary may have changed at some point.

Dad was born on New Year's Day in 1875. Although he was my grandmother's[xvi] third son, he was the first child born after his parents' 1874 marriage. My father had seven brothers and two sisters, but his eldest brother, James William Edgar Alker, was always referred to as his step-brother because he was born before his mother married. His second oldest brother, Arthur, was also born out of wedlock, but he was never referred to as a step-brother. I have no idea why unless it was because he had the same father as the other children of the marriage. The other brothers were Arthur, Samuel, Alfred, Stanley, Herbert and Thomas. His sisters were Elizabeth and Margaret. My Alker grandparents were William Alker and Jane Edgar.

After my father married my mother, there was a lot of talk that he'd married beneath him. I'm not sure of the exact reasons, but it could have been because she was 19 years younger than he was, and she was working as a barmaid. The fact she became pregnant by him before they were married also probably went against her. It was around this time that he ceased working on his father's farm and went to work for his cousin John Alker.[xvii]

Wanting to marry my mother, my father had asked his dad for a wage increase. His dad refused. So while dad became a farm labourer at Chapel Street Farm, his two younger brothers, Thomas and Stanley, took over the running of Mellings Farm. Their other brother, Samuel, also had a hand in the farms management, but he lived and worked mainly in Buenos Aries. Sam had gained a Bachelor of Science, Honours Degree in Agriculture at Preston, and was employed as a Biochemist for a forestry firm called La Forestal in Argentina. Samuel never married, nor did his brother Stanley, nor his sister Elizabeth.

Of dad's other siblings, Arthur had married a lady called Mary Richardson, Herbert's wife was called Ann, Thomas had married Ellen Peel (Nelly) and Margaret had married a farmer called James Turner.[xviii] They were living in Windy Arbour farm in Winstanley. Dad's stepbrother, James William Edgar Alker, was always known as William. He married and had two sets of twins: two girls called Jenny and Bessie, and two boys called William and Alfred. There was also a daughter called Marie. Alfred, the only brother of my dad I haven't mentioned, went to live in St Asaph, Wales. I only know he lived there because when he died, sometime during the War in 1941, I received a copy of his will because he left me £200. I now know he did marry a lady called Emily Foster. She died before him in 1933.[xix] The address given at the time of her death was Rock Cottage, Tremeirchion, North Wales.

These were my father's brothers and sisters. I was also acquainted with some of their children, my cousins. For instance, Uncle Tom and Auntie Nelly had a daughter called Kathleen. She was a bit younger than me. We used to spend time together whenever I went to the farm to stay with my grandfather,

My mother never really got on with Tom and his wife. I think the way they treated her later affected my feelings towards them. Tom and Nelly always managed to make my mother feel beneath them but, thinking back, it went deeper than that. Perhaps seeing my mother reminded them of the things they'd done to her. I'd seen them borrowing money from her on a regular basis. Usually it was ten shillings, money mother could ill afford, but she was kind hearted.

I remember Uncle Sam coming back from Argentina on a visit. He had his own sitting room at Mellings farm that wasn't used by the rest of the family, and he just came out for meals. It was always drilled into me that he was not to be disturbed. When he did eventually come out of his sitting room, he wore a smoking jacket; it was velvet and seemed very elaborate. As a child I was definitely in awe of him.

I don't know what impressions he picked up from the family when he was home, but I do know he subsequently went out of his way to help my father and mother when they were ill. He used to pay for my father's medicine and have it shipped from Argentina.

My father used to say that Sam thought a lot of my mother. Even after father died, my uncle continued to help my mum. Then after she'd passed on, he continued to help me. I still have a couple of the letters he sent me from Villa Guillamina, Santa Fe, Argentina. In one he asks all about George, what he did for a living and whether we were provided for adequately. He often enclosed money in the envelope, and when we were at war, he provided me with a regular income. So there I was with George's increased war pay, my weekly wage from Chivers, and my two pounds a month from good old Uncle Sam.

SOME GOOD TIMES

Brian had now settled in school very well. Although, when I'd left him the first day, he ran all around the school yard with the teacher chasing after him.

As they ran past me she shouted, "Leave him Mrs Smith! He'll be alright." And he was too!

In Chivers, I was relegated to sorting strawberries for the jam, but that was only a starting position and I eventually moved on through the different rooms. I enjoyed the work and made many friends. There was one special friend in the canning room. Her name escapes me at the moment, but we shared the same sense of humour and had many a giggle there. We both started in the canning room together and all I remember about that room was all the water. We were supposed to wear rubber aprons and clogs but, being fashion conscious young ladies, we didn't want to wear clogs. We refused, point blank, to have anything to do with them, so we were sent off to see the factory nurse to see what she had to say about it. She soon talked us round, and we spent the next hour laughing at ourselves and the way we looked.

After finishing work each evening at half past five, we had quite a long walk home. One Friday evening I came out of the gates alone and a strange woman came up to me. She spun me some story about being an evacuee from London and having several children who she had to get back to, but she had no money. She said if I lent her the money she'd repay me. I had just received my weekly wage of two pounds and seven shillings. How green can you get? Me being me, I just handed my wage packet over, unopened, not even thinking she hadn't asked me where she could send the money to. Of course I never heard from her again. I felt so stupid about it later that I didn't tell George or anyone else for that matter but, eventually, I did tell and it's been a family joke ever since. I'm the soft one who gave her wages away.

Another funny episode at Chivers involved the mincemeat room. This room was only opened in September of every year in preparation for the Christmas mince pies. The mincemeat used to travel down a chute from the room above. When the worker in our room was ready for the mincemeat they had to flick a switch. This set off a red light in the room above and the workers there would send down the mincemeat through a large funnel. As soon as we had enough mincemeat we were supposed to flick the switch off right away. One afternoon, one of the girls got distracted and forgot to flick off her switch and the stuff just kept pouring down the funnel. She was absolutely covered in mincemeat, and the rest of us laughed so much we were in hysterics. The following day the same thing happened to me and we all fell about laughing again.

There was a really lovely atmosphere in Chivers. It was a great place to work. They played records for us every afternoon, and then Friday afternoon would be request time. Once, I had a lovely surprise when the girls had my song played for me. It was Vera Lynn singing 'Yours' and was special for me and George. I made lots of friends there and, for the most part, I was able to keep my mind off the war and all its horrors. Being in Cambridge we were close to an air-field and you could hear the aeroplanes going over but, thankfully, there was no sound of bombing.

Mrs Thulbourne had a married daughter called Greta who had a baby. On my days off, I used to take the baby out. Sometimes Greta and I would go around the market together. It was a really lovely feeling to have money in my pocket and I could now buy some of the things we wanted as long as I had the right coupons. The Thulbourne's also had a small dog which I also took out, usually to the large playing field in the middle of the housing estate. The men from the forces would always be playing football there whenever I passed with the dog. Now and again in the evening, we would all go to a concert held in the community hall. It was called 'Impington Hall'.[xx] All the neighbours would go too and I made many friends.

Time passed and George was now due for another leave. We decided we'd have to go home to Liverpool to see how things were at Woodbine Grove.

Before we were due to leave Cambridge, I asked my sister-in-law Hannah if she'd like to come to Cambridge for a short holiday. Of course I'd already cleared it first with Mrs Thulbourne. Hannah was elated and spent the last two weeks with me in Cambridge before I left. I was able to take her around the jam factory and show her all the places I found so interesting. It was a very sad day when we had to leave Mrs Thulbourne and her family. She'd been like a mother to me and we'd become very close. I was given many going away presents, some only given as I was about to board the train. Everyone was so kind. Hannah travelled home with me and although I was eager to get home and see George and all my old Liverpool friends, I was also sad at leaving.

LATTER WAR YEARS

Whenever I'd been away, I'd continued to send my rent to my landlady May for our two rooms. I didn't know it at the time, but we were paying far more for those rooms than we should have. May was renting the house off the real landlord for ten shillings per week, yet she was charging us ten shillings for just two rooms.

Back in Liverpool, everything seemed so strange. After all, we'd been away over twelve months. I had left our rooms open so that May could light a fire in there every so often but, sadly, she never bothered. The rooms had become so damp, that our lovely three piece suite was going mouldy underneath the cushions. I could have cried, especially when I remembered how much money I had been regularly sending her. It wasn't long before I discovered another lodger had come to live in the house during my absence. Mrs Williams, a very old lady in her late seventies, had been given a small back room where she lived and slept. She was unaware that George and I had been living there prior to her arrival, and consequently seemed surprised to find us coming and going, much as we were to discover her.

Despite the surprise of finding a stranger in the house, we soon settled down again and I made the arrangements for Brian to attend Boaler Street School.

George came home on leave shortly after I'd arrived home and he went to see his old employer, Mr Anakin. As a result of this, Mr Anakin decided to pay George one Pound every fortnight. It was his way of making sure George went back to work for him after the war. He valued George highly because George had been with him as a young boy of fourteen and had worked his way up to being a trusted long distance lorry driver. We always felt a bit uncomfortable taking this money, especially since we knew George was the only ex-employee receiving a handout from him, but the money was useful so we were grateful.

After Cambridge, I never went away with George again while he was serving in the army. Instead, I concentrated on making friends with my neighbours in Liverpool. I had a very good friend living next door, a Mrs Whitter. She was a lot older than me, and we used to cry on each other's shoulders whenever things got us down, and that was often.

I got to know May a little better too. All this time she was still working in the theatre. She often told me about her younger days and how she wanted to become a nun. She'd courted a young man while in her teens, but the urge to become a nun had been so strong, she'd decided to give him up.

One day I opened the front door to a strange man who wanted to see May. When I explained she was at work, he left her a note. Later, May introduced him as the young man she'd courted. His wife had died and he had a young son. It wasn't long before she was looking after the young boy while his dad went to work. One Saturday, just three months after they'd met up again, May said that she was getting married to him that very day and we never saw her again. She just left the house as it was. Her dishes and other belongings were still in the cupboards, and everything else left just as she'd last used it. We had a terrible time sorting out the mess she'd left behind because she was never one for housework.

However, it was the old lady, Mrs Williams, who worried me most. As the first weekend without May approached, she handed me a rent book and ten shillings. I was amazed that she had been paying ten shillings to May too, and for just one poky little room, much less space than I had. As well as living rent free, May had been making a tidy profit from us.

I refused to take that much off the old lady and told her this, but she became annoyed with me and insisted I take it. That's what it said on her rent book and she didn't want it spoiled, she explained. Well no matter how hard I tried to tell her she shouldn't be paying all that, she insisted she would, so I ended up taking the ten shillings. Not for long though because, unhappy with the situation, I went to see Mrs William's granddaughter who lived in our street, and in the end she took her grandmother in.

We now had this large house to ourselves. It was very spacious, having four rooms downstairs and four rooms upstairs, but it was also in very bad repair. Everywhere was damp. May had never bothered to tell the landlord; probably because she was afraid he'd find out she was subletting. The poor state of the house depressed me so much that, in the end, I contacted the landlord and asked him to do something about it.

By this time, George was about to go on another course to help him during the second attempt at France. It was a worrying time for us all, hoping that our loved ones would return safely to us. In February 1943, George came home on leave. We were luckier than most really because at least he was still in England while many of his friends had been posted abroad. There were many times in those days when every song that came out had a special meaning to couples like us. I remember one evening in particular, when George was sitting in his armchair and I was sitting on the floor at his feet. We were both in tears listening to the lyrics of 'Night and Day' on the radio. It was soul destroying for us both when he had to go back to the barracks, especially after the bliss of being home on leave. Those were the worst times.

It wasn't long after this particular leave that I realised I was pregnant. I was so happy and I knew George would be over the moon about it too. We'd been talking about another baby for a long time but, somehow, it hadn't happened until Brian was nearly seven.

Being on my own most of the time, George and I thought it would be a good idea for me to go to his mother's home in Pemberton for the birth. This had been my mother's home before she died so I knew I'd feel comfortable there and went just a few weeks before my due time. Brian had been a pre-war baby and now I was to have a war baby. I kept very well all through my pregnancy and George always said I was at my best then, but I suppose lots of women are.

Our second son, Victor William Smith, was born at quarter past three one Wednesday afternoon in 1943. My mother-in law[xxi] always loved to listen to Victor Sylvester on the radio and wanted the baby to be called

Sylvia if it was a girl. So seeing we'd had a boy, I thought she'd be pleased if we called him Victor. William is George's second name and also his father's first name. Our son was beautiful with lovely golden coloured hair. He was darker than Brian who was very blonde. At that time George was stationed in Rhyl and a telegram was sent to him, so he was allowed to come home on leave again for a few days.

Unfortunately, having a war baby meant that everything I bought had to be utility. The baby prams at that time were really ugly. The one I had was so deep; I had to pile pillows in it before I could put the baby in. Otherwise you couldn't see him. I did manage to get him a lovely wicker cot though, and all the other things we needed for a new baby. After a few weeks in Pemberton, when I'd regained my strength, we returned home to Liverpool.

Knowing it was more difficult for me to get about now I had two children; my two sisters-in-law came to visit me more often. One particular day, Hannah came by herself. After arriving in Liverpool and walking along London Road, she met someone who was later to become her husband.

After courting him for a while she would often say to me, "I hope when I marry, I'm as happy as you and George."

George went over to France in June 1944. I heard from him quite often whenever he had the chance to write, but all letters were censored from then on, so I never knew which part of France he was in. Whenever I replied to his letters I always had to address them to 'Somewhere in France'.

In July, when George had only been in France a few weeks, I received a telegram to say my husband had been wounded. I hadn't heard from him since he went to France and had been very worried. Obviously, when I received the telegram, I was frantic. I remember crying and running to my neighbour, Mrs Whitter. The telegram said George had been wounded in the head, no more and no less. Of course, I was thinking the worst. Maybe he'd lose his memory and not know me, or perhaps he'd be permanently brain damaged. It was a terrible time not knowing exactly what was wrong, and worrying about how much this injury would affect our marriage.

It wasn't too long before he was well enough to write and tell me himself what had happened. He'd been hit in the head by shrapnel. At first, when he'd seen his helmet on the floor, he thought he'd been foolish and forgotten to wear it, but on picking it up and seeing the hole through it, he realised it had been blown off his head with the force. Fortunately, the shrapnel had only grazed him. How lucky can you get? Someone must have been watching over him that day.

As usual, we carried on writing to each other, but everything had to be so secretive. George was not allowed to tell me anything that was going on.

Hannah was married in August of that year. John, her husband, was a regular in the army and had served most of his time in India, so for the rest of his time in the army, he was stationed quite near home. As they had nowhere to live, I agreed they could come and live with me and the children on the understanding they found somewhere else before George came home on leave. They soon found more permanent rooms near where we lived, and Hannah used to come and see me often, even to the point of doing her washing at our place.

Sadly, I soon learned that her marriage wasn't as happy as she'd hoped it would be. John loved to go dancing and to the clubs, often going on his own while Hannah was looking after their baby girl. Later, they decided to go back and live with her parents in Pemberton for a while. By that time, her mum and dad only had their youngest daughter, Dorothy, at home.

Meanwhile, I was busy having repairs done to the house whenever I could get anyone out. All the able bodied men were in the forces so it was difficult, yet certain jobs had to be done. The roof had been neglected for years and was letting in rain in our bedroom. The raids had eased off by now, and we were sleeping in our own beds again, so I thought it would be nice if the rooms were dry and not always damp. I did manage to get someone to see to it, but it didn't make any difference as it still leaked, though not quite as much as before.

I had my work cut out looking after the two children. Brian, who was at school, was very mischievous and needed to be watched constantly. It was lucky for me that Victor was such a good baby.

Even the workmen who were seeing to the house commented on it, saying, "I've never seen such a contented baby." Victor would be just sitting in his pram happily watching them.

In March 1945, George came home on leave from France and was able to tell me more of what had been happening over there. I was so grateful that he'd not been more seriously wounded. He was now even able to laugh about it, telling me he'd called himself a stupid fool when he thought he'd forgotten to wear his helmet. He did try to bring that tin helmet home but he wasn't able to.

We considered ourselves very lucky during these war years for we did get to spend quite a bit of time together compared to other couples. Now we were longing for the war to be over so we could get on with our lives. George would often discuss what he'd do about his job when the war finally ended. He intended getting a better one with more money. I heard him say this so often, it made me feel guilty, for I was still taking ten shillings a week from his old boss, Mr Anakin. So when George's leave was over and he'd returned to the army, I stopped taking that money. I did miss it, but at least I no longer felt guilty about it. Within a few weeks of George leaving, I soon realised I was pregnant for the third time, and hoped for a little girl. During this pregnancy, George came back from France and was stationed in Woolwich awaiting his demob.

This time I decided to stay home for my confinement. Hannah, my sister-in-law promised to come down and look after the two boys when I went into labour. The day before the baby was due George came home on leave again. It was a very quick delivery compared to my other two pregnancies. I was only in labour for just over an hour when baby Carole made her appearance into the world. We were delighted we now had a baby girl. We had a pre-war baby, a war baby, and now a peace baby. Just one thing was missing—although the fighting was over, I was still waiting for George to be demobbed so we could all be together.

GETTING BACK TO NORMAL

Early in 1946, my husband finally came home for good. It was a very happy time, not only for me but for everyone else too. At last the war was over. There were street parties all over the country and everyone seemed to be your friend. There was a wonderful feeling of friendship and caring that people had built up over those bleak war years. Everyone had love and feelings for each other and supported each other as best they could.[xxii]

After a short rest and a lot of talking, George did go back to his old job hoping to get something better later on when things had settled down more. It wasn't long after this when we both realised George wasn't as well as we'd thought. He seemed to be suffering with his nerves. It was the after affects of war trauma I expect.

For the next twelve months, he had to attend the Royal Infirmary in Liverpool for electric shock treatment, and I had to go with him. It was awful to see him after his treatment. He would be just like a baby having to be told what to do next, not at all his usual capable self. It was a very worrying time for us.

His employer was very understanding and gave him ample time off work, so when George did get well again, he was reluctant to let him down by seeking alternative employment like he'd planned. Consequently, he ended up staying with Mr Anakin for several years after he'd fully recovered.

Unfortunately, although George was in regular work, his pay was rather low. It was only a small company, and his boss couldn't afford to pay high wages. Our salvation at this time was the two pounds a month I was still receiving from my Uncle Sam. He was the only one from my father's side of the family who ever showed any concern for me, and I was grateful. Over the years, I did visit a few other members of my father's family. His brother Tom was one and also his sister Lizzie, but they never mentioned Uncle Sam, so I'm afraid I didn't either.

For a long time, we muddled through as best we could without me working. Then, when Carole was about three years old, George and I had some words over the lack of money. The outcome of this led to me seeking a job outside the home.

It was a freezing cold January day when I went out looking for work, and I was determined that I'd find some. I trampled all over the town centre that day visiting various cafes and cinemas. In one café the manageress told me to go home, as she thought that particular café was no place for a girl like me. I had to admit it did look rough. I don't suppose I would have lasted five minutes there.

Feeling dejected, I caught the tram home and, as fate would have it, on the journey home I met an acquaintance, a girl who was related to my friend Peggy from years before. I told her I'd been out looking for a part-time job and, lo and behold, she told me to go to the Royal cinema on Breck Road, which wasn't too far from where I lived. She knew that three girls had just been sacked there and they'd probably be looking for staff. It was to be my lucky day after all because I went right away and was taken on there.

From then on, each evening, I went out to work at five thirty in the afternoon just as George returned home from work. Not the ideal situation, I know, but money became less of a problem and we started to enjoy life again, even having occasional days out.

Sometimes, if the weather was fine, we'd take a trip to Moreton where there was a large playing field and a long breakwater to stroll along. We'd take some sandwiches and buy a cup of tea. Even though we'd have to catch a tram to the Pier Head, cross the river Mersey by ferry, and then catch another tram to Moreton, the fares were very cheap, only a few coppers really.

Those were the days! The only thing that spoiled it for us was the fact I had to be in work by late afternoon, so I often left George and the children there while I made my own way back. George used to laugh about it later, telling me how the children used to run all over the ferry with him in anxious pursuit. George proved himself to be a wonderful father. He had so much patience with the children and, of course, he was the one to put them to bed every night.

Needless to say, like most people we did have our little problems as the children were growing up. One particular little episode I remember well, was some trouble with one of Carole's little friends. They would play together fine until slides and ribbons started to go missing from Carole's hair. Nothing to get upset over, but George got tired of this sort of thing. He decided to have a chat with the girl's mother to see if she could talk to her daughter about it. When the child's mother answered the door and he'd explained why he was there, she called her husband to the door.

George was astounded when she then ordered her husband, "Get stuck in."

He did, and the next thing George knew they were both rolling about and fighting in the street. My husband had never been an aggressive man. He was not really lashing out, but was concentrating on shielding himself from the blows the other man was delivering. Anyway, someone shouted for the police, so they broke it up and George came home.

Later, after the other man had time to cool down, George went to see how he was and they ended up shaking hands. When I finished work that night, George was waiting for me outside the cinema with a terrible black eye. He told me what had happened, and said he was worried in case they stopped me on my way home from work as I had to pass their door.

When we were home, I became concerned about his eye and decided he needed some ointment for it. Unfortunately, the only open chemist shop was in Lime Street, a tram ride away. So although George was against me going out at that time of night, I went to get some ointment.

On the way to Lime Street, I felt growing apprehension. I feared I had made a mistake going out after all. Lime Street was noted for being a bad part of Liverpool, famous for its prostitutes. Sitting next to me on the tram was a young fellow, and I noticed he was looking at me. In the end, he asked me where I was going.

"To the chemist in Lime Street," I told him.

As I got off the tram, he did too. He told me not to worry, that this was no place for a young person like me on her own, and he'd see me to the chemist and then back onto the tram home. He was as good as his word, funny how you could trust people in those days. I was most grateful to him, and when I returned home I told George all about him.

Next day, in the bread shop, I met the little girl's mother and she said, "I didn't know your husband could fight like that."

I replied, "No, you wouldn't, because he's so quiet."

There was no further trouble after that, and the children continued playing with each other.

Shortly after this, Victor had an accident and had to be taken to hospital. It was a Sunday morning and the two boys were having a pillow fight on the bed. Suddenly, there was a terrific scream. We raced upstairs to find Victor had fallen off the bed and cut his eye on the corner of the bedding box. He was in a terrible state. We bound his head with a towel and George carried him to hospital. He still has a scar over his eye to this day.

Being an usherette was often boring work, particularly if there was a poor film showing and few customers came in. I was getting on well, so after three years I was made relief cashier, and when one of the full timers left, I was given her job.

The extra money came in very handy, and the following year we were able to take a proper holiday. One of Carole's friends had an aunt who owned a caravan in North Wales, and she asked us if we'd like to hire it for a week. We were delighted to take up the offer as it was quite cheap. We travelled by coach and upon reaching our destination; George went off to find the caravan while the children and I waited with the heavy cases.

After a while he came back. Seeming despondent, he said, "I think you're going to be disappointed love."

True enough, I was. The caravan looked more like a small hut on wheels and was called 'Uncle Tom's Cabin'. Inside, it was filthy, and we had to clean it out from top to bottom before we could even unpack the suitcases. By the time we'd finished, I felt as if I'd only been put on this earth to clean up after other people. Once the cleaning had been done and forgotten about though, we did really have a lovely week's holiday.

On the Saturday morning, after we'd been there a week, the lady who owned the caravan came as we were getting ready to leave. She passed remarks about how clean the van looked and suggested we could stop another week if we wanted to.

"I'm sorry," I said, "but we don't have the money."

"Oh, that's alright." she replied, "You can pay me later."

We didn't stay. I can remember saying to George, "If ever we have a caravan, I'll make sure it's always clean."

I didn't know it then, but shortly after this we were able to buy our own little caravan.

TURNING POINT IN OUR LIVES

It all came about in the early fifties when Uncle Sam died. His solicitor, in London, sent us a copy of his will. He'd never married and had left quite a tidy sum, eleven thousand pounds in all.[xxiii] This was to be divided up between his nieces and nephews. The only snag was the inheritance didn't come into effect until Uncle Sam's sister, Elizabeth, died. She was a spinster, and was receiving an income from the interest the estate was making. Well, we were really excited at the prospect of that windfall but, little did we know, it would be more than twenty years later before we would actually receive it. It was very unsettling in a way, knowing you've been left a large amount of money, yet not actually having received it. My Aunt Lizzie was almost seventy at this time and, although we didn't discuss it, we presumed we wouldn't have too long to wait, so we often daydreamed about how we were going to spend it.

As time went on, we decided we would like a small caravan for our holidays. We were both working and knew we could afford a loan. By this time, I'd given up my cinema work in favour of full time work, so we went to have a look at some caravans in Wales. Looking back, I suppose we could have arranged it better, but we agreed to pay only interest on the loan. The full amount we borrowed would be paid back when my inheritance was realised, a matter of just a few years, we thought.

We chose a reconditioned caravan. It had been in a fire and had been almost entirely rebuilt. It had new roofing, side panels and internal fittings. It was a lovely little van, coach built and just right for our needs. The loan was also enough for George to buy a second hand car and all the little extras we needed for the van.

We sited it at Talacre, North Wales, and what fun we had. Talacre was nicknamed 'Little Liverpool', and rightly so because there were lots of Liverpudlians who holidayed there. We made many new friends on our weekends in Wales. George couldn't finish work quickly enough on Friday afternoons; such was his haste to be off for the weekends.

Looking back, I often wonder how I coped. My new job was in the local sweet factory, Barker and Dobson. It was close enough to enable me to get back home at lunch time. If I hurried, there was just enough time for me to collect a few messages on the way home and then grab a bite to eat before I had to get back to work for the afternoon. The job itself was much harder than I'd been used to before. I was employed in the boiler room, where the men boiled the toffee before pouring it onto hot slabs. Three other girls and I had the job of turning the toffee until it was ready to be made into a particular sweet. The supervisor was in the same section as me so that whenever a new variety of sweet came out, we were the first to produce it. I quite enjoyed the work, but it could be very dangerous as one splash of hot toffee could give you a very nasty burn. There was always someone wearing a bandage. I had to wear one myself a few times. Eventually, I was put on a machine that made all the centres, such as chocolate for the éclairs, or jam. I worked on a slab a little bit apart from the others and as the men poured the chocolate out on the bench, I would get it to the right texture and put it on a tray. The chocolate was then put into the centre of the toffee, folded up, then put onto rollers and threaded through the chocolate éclair machine. All the different varieties of the sweets started off in much the same way, having boiling toffee poured out onto hot slabs. We could vary the heat on these slabs, cooling them if necessary. The heat made it very tiring work, especially in summer.

Most days I would get home from work just a few minutes before George and so I would start the tea. After we'd eaten, I'd have all the household chores to do. No washing machine for me in those days. I had to do the laundry all by hand and reserved Monday evenings for this job. Then of course, there was ironing, shopping, and a million other little things that needed to be done in the house. George did help as much as he could and made the task of washing the dishes his job. He also put the children to bed while I got on with the other tasks.

At first, I loved going to the caravan every weekend but, as time passed, this also became a chore. I would get annoyed when George inevitably asked, "Will you be ready to go to the caravan on Friday?"

All I seemed to do when we were there was clean the darned thing. We were beginning to take bookings for it, and I had to be sure it was nice enough for people to holiday in it. George often took the clients down there in our car, and then took the people, who were already there, home. Renting the caravan out and ferrying people to and fro helped to pay for the ground rent and also the interest on the loan, both of which increased every year.

I soon found that working through the day had its drawbacks as well as its advantages. Although I was now seeing far more of my husband, I felt a bit uneasy about not being there for the children when they came home from school. Brian, the eldest, had just started work as an errand boy for Woodson's grocery store on West Derby Road, but the other two children were still relatively young. Carole, the youngest, must have been about six when I'd changed jobs and Victor would have been eight.

They used to go to an after school activity centre to fill in the time until I got home. This was held at Boaler Street School. I never knew what would be facing me after work. One particular neighbour would often pull me up over Brian, telling me everything he'd been up to. I used to dread seeing her on my return, and often felt like packing my job in because of this, but we couldn't have managed without the money.

One day, after I'd been getting onto Brian over something this neighbour had just told me, he turned on me and said, "Mum, don't you know why she picks on me?"

"No. Why?" I replied.

"It's because you take notice of her and the other mum's don't."

I realised then he was right, yet I still felt guilty leaving them. I suppose we could have got by without my wage but we couldn't have had the car and caravan, and seeing the children enjoying their trips to Wales made it all seem worthwhile.

All this time, we were still living in the same old house in Woodbine Grove. I suppose most people today would say, "Why didn't you buy a house instead of a caravan and car?"

Believe me; we never even gave it a thought. Nobody we knew had bought their own house. Besides, there were plenty of properties available to rent. As the years passed, we travelled all over Wales exploring the various areas using Talacre as our base.

Brian was about sixteen when he started courting. At first, when he started staying out late, we were worried because we didn't know where he was. Once he'd explained, we were able to relax a bit more, although I still didn't like him coming in too late. I would lie in bed worrying until I heard him come in. Eventually, we had an invitation to his girlfriend's twenty first birthday party. Joan, his girlfriend was four years older than Brian. Once we'd met her and her family we knew he was alright. Soon afterwards, they got engaged and just before Brian's twentieth birthday, they were married. They lived with us for about two years, and then Brian went to work for the I.C.I. in Cheshire because they had houses for the workers to rent. So they moved down there and eventually bought their own house there.

Carole was eleven years old when Brian and Joan got married. She had always been bright but had not passed the eleven-plus exam. At thirteen, she tried for the thirteen-plus scholarship and this time passed.

Although she had wanted to go to technical college, there was a mix up somewhere along the line, and she was sent to Holly Lodge grammar school. She'd always enjoyed school up to that point, but from then on, she disliked it and started to rebel. In the grammar school, it seemed that the girls who passed at thirteen were somehow seen as inferior to the mainstream pupils who had entered the school at eleven years old. Carole said they were treated differently. I do know that all the lessons she enjoyed, like art and needlework, had to be given up until her thirteen-plus class had caught up with the rest of the thirteen year olds in maths and English. Anyway, by the time she was sixteen, she was pestering us because she wanted to leave. She was supposed to stay on until the end of the summer term but she wanted to leave at Easter. We could see she was unhappy there so in the end we gave in, knowing we'd have to pay for her to leave early.

Finally, we said, "If you find yourself a job you can leave."

She immediately found herself work in sewing and left school at Easter. It cost us ten pounds, but it was worth every penny to see her happy again. From then on, she started to make a lot of her own clothes and seemed to be doing alright for herself.

Victor left school at fifteen. Like Brian he'd gone to Newsham Secondary Modern. At first he seemed to have a bit of trouble finding a job. One day, during my lunch break, I went into the local greengrocers on West Derby Road. It was Anakin's and belonged to the firm George used to work for. By this time George was working in Chorley and travelling there every day.

There were workmen in the shop doing some painting, so just as a joke really, I asked if there were any jobs going in their firm.

I told them about Victor and one of them said, "Send him down to the office. There may be something for him."

Victor did go down and was taken on as an apprentice painter and decorator. The firm was called Fairclough and, as far as I know, was in Juvenal Street.

As I've stated before, our house was in a very bad condition, but so were the majority of the others in that particular neighbourhood. They were all very old. They had been condemned by the council as unfit for habitation many years before, so they were due to be pulled down.

By the year 1962, some of our neighbours had already been re-housed. My good friend Mrs Whitter from next door had already gone, and the council were in a hurry to re-house us too. My neighbours on the other side, also good friends, were reluctant to move. They were George and Winnie Rogerson who had no children, just a cat. George had a van covered in advertisements for crisps. It was the only vehicle in our street before we bought our little car.

When the council made us an offer of a flat in Kirkby, George and Winnie came with us to view it. They begged us not to take it, asking us to hold out as long as we could.

We didn't need much persuading to refuse that particular flat because while we were looking it over, the man in the flat immediately opposite came out and said, "I wouldn't come here if I were you, Pal; we've got nine kids here and another on the way."

Needless to say, we beat a hasty retreat. When the next offer came, we were told it would be the last, so we had to take it. This was also a flat but in a much nicer place than the first. It overlooked Lord Derby's estate and was in Silverwell Road, Croxteth.

Although we would have preferred a house, we soon settled into the flat, and what bliss it was to have a bathroom at long last. We hadn't even had a hot tap in Woodbine Grove. We'd thought it a luxury when George installed an electric light in the outside toilet. Now we were living in luxury.

We'd always been reluctant to spend money on doing up the old house and, for years, anything we'd bought was saved for when we moved. Now, at last, we had moved, and we discarded most of our old furniture and bought all new.

After we'd been in the new property twelve months, Carole decided to seek work nearer where we lived. She'd been working in Colquitt Street, in the town centre and was now finding the travelling tedious. The problem was the excessive time it took to get to and from work in the peak hours. She found a sewing job nearby and settled down again. This time she was working for J and P Jacob, a clothing factory commonly known as 'The Paula Works'. It was near Stopgate Lane. By this time she had begun courting.

I was still travelling to my work in Barker and Dobson. It wasn't quite as far to travel as the city centre but, nevertheless, I was getting fed up of the travelling also. Soon after we'd moved, I remember being late for work one morning. It was winter and the mornings were very dark. I had to leave about quarter past seven, and went as usual to the bus stop which also served as a bus terminus. Since arriving in the district, I'd only ever seen a number fourteen bus at that stop, so I jumped on the bus just leaving without checking the number. It was only when I found myself in strange surroundings, I realised I must have been on the wrong bus. I was nearly at the docks in Liverpool by then. I'd started to panic because I knew I would be late for work. It was well after nine o' clock when I turned up. You can bet I never made that mistake again.

Another bad moment happened, at a later date, as I was getting ready for work. I'd had new dentures fitted and suddenly developed lockjaw. I'd had it once or twice before since I'd had my new teeth, but this time it wouldn't go back and was very painful.

Wrapping a scarf around my mouth I headed off to the local doctors. We were not registered with him at this time, but I thought he'd see me. It was only about seven o' clock in the morning, and when he answered the door, I tried to tell him what was wrong—difficult when you can't move your jaw. He wouldn't help me though, as I wasn't his patient. He just told me to go to my own doctor who was in Sheil Road. I was waiting at the bus stop for the bus that would take me there when, suddenly, the lockjaw disappeared. I ended up just going back home where I finished getting ready for work. I've never had it since but I had an uncle who had it a lot, so I must have taken after him.

Carole came home one day and told me she'd arranged an interview for me at her place of work, so I went the next day. I was taken on in the warehouse as a packer with the understanding that if I proved my worth, I would take over as supervisor in two years time when the present supervisor retired. I'd never been ambitious, but I wasn't too worried about this future responsibility because I presumed I'd have probably left the firm by then. However, it was a nice clean job and I got on well with all the other girls there, especially Flo, the supervisor. It was much easier working nearer to home and since George had also changed his job, he began picking Carole and I up in the car after we'd all finished work. George was working for the Lucas Company now, at English Electric. It was on the East Lancashire Road, not far at all from where we now lived.

All this time, Victor was still seeing his friend from our old neighbourhood. Unbelievably, he was the brother of the little girl who used to take Carole's hair slides. They had been friends for many years and now they were older they both had lovely new motorbikes and used to go everywhere together on them. This seemed to aggravate some of the boys in our new area. I suppose they thought Victor should have mixed more with them, but he was quite happy with his old friend's company. One snowy winter, his bike was stolen and, at the time, we believed the thief was somebody local.

It was now about 1964. I was at work one day when the Personnel Officer came in the warehouse to see me. It turned out my eldest son Brian had been involved in an accident at work and was now in hospital;

69

apparently, he'd somehow knocked his head on one of the machines.

I decided not to tell Carole who, of course, was working in the design room of the same factory. There was no point in worrying everyone until we knew the severity of the situation. George came to collect me, and we picked up Brian's wife, Joan, from where she lived in Weaverham, near Northwich in Cheshire, and took her to Whiston hospital where Brian had been taken. A few weeks later, Brian was discharged. He later developed Multiple Sclerosis and we'll never know if the knock to his head had anything to do with it.

It was about this time Victor started seeing a young lady who'd been taken on in the office of his firm. He brought her home to meet us, and she told him she was from Australia and was only staying here for two years. She came over with her parents and her sister and intended going back with them when the two years were up. Her name was Vivian, and she told us she already had a steady boyfriend in Australia. They intended getting married when she returned.

Victor thought a lot of her and respected her all the more for telling him that. After a while she grew fond of my son, but said that she couldn't make up her mind until she'd been back to see Philip, her boyfriend.

Her parents, Mr and Mrs Sheehan, were lovely people too and told Victor that if he wanted to emigrate he was welcome to stay with them, regardless of who Vivian ended up with. Victor had already told them he was thinking of doing just that, as it was an idea he'd been toying with for a couple of years.

When the Sheehan's eventually went back to Australia they continued to keep in touch with Victor by letter. Vivian decided to marry her boyfriend, Philip, but said Victor would be welcome to stay at her parent's house for as long as he wanted. Such generous people!

Later that year, Victor left England bound for Australia on an assisted passage, just twelve months after the Sheehan's had left. He was just twenty one; and I thought I'd never get over it. We heard from him regularly, but each letter broke my heart. He was so far away and I thought I'd never see him again.

He seemed to be doing well: finding work, making lots of new friends, even holidaying in Bali, and of course being looked after by the Sheehan family. Vivian and her sister Lorraine helped him in his appearance so that he wouldn't look too much like a green pommie when he went out and about. I shall be eternally grateful to them all for looking after him and setting him off on the right foot.

It was now coming up to the time when I was due to be made supervisor. I didn't relish the idea at all as I was quite happy just being one of the girls. When I was subsequently called into the office and reminded of my obligation, I refused it at first; but the manager boosted my confidence and persuaded me to accept the extra responsibility. When Flo finally left, I took her place. In reality, it wasn't that much different to what I'd been doing before. It was only if something went wrong I needed to take charge and put it right, and by then I'd had enough experience at the job to know what had to be done.

Just a couple of months before Victor emigrated; Carole married her boyfriend, Mike, who she'd been courting for two years. They stayed with us for the first couple of years while they looked for somewhere to live. It wasn't easy, but Mike then found work in the New Town of Skelmersdale and they were given a council house there. They'd already had two babies by now, both boys, with less than fourteen months between them.

TIME FOR OUSELVES

At last, George and I were on our own. We still had the caravan but it was now starting to get old, and the owner of the site in Talacre wanted to modernise by getting rid of all the older and smaller vans. George eventually moved our van to a farm some miles away while we decided what to do about it. The farmer used to go fishing in Lake Coniston and asked if he could buy it off us. We were pleased to have it taken off our hands if the truth was known. It had become a liability with the ever increasing ground rent, so we were pleased to see the back of it even though we were still paying interest on the loan that we'd taken out to buy it. Yes, after all this time, we were still waiting for Uncle Sam's bequest to be settled. It had been seventeen years ago when we first heard about it. Eventually, we sold the caravan to the farmer.

Our holidays, from then on, became more adventurous. We went to explore Cornwall, Devon and in later years even took our little car abroad to tour France, Spain, Monaco, and other exotic destinations. Mainly, for these excursions, we holidayed in a tent which gave us a new sense of freedom.

Several years later, found our little family geographically split up, but still close in our hearts. Brian and Joan now had three children, Andrew, Pauline, and Martin, and were still living in their little ex-council house in Weaverham, but now they owned it. Although Brian was still working, he'd been given an easier job so that his increasing inability to walk didn't affect his job.

Victor was now living in Australia with his wife, Robyn, and their two children, Shane and Mark. A third child was on the way. A few years after emigrating, my son had opened his own painting and decorating business employing several people, but he was now studying real estate. His father-in-law owned his own real estate business, and wanted Victor and his own son, Paul, to eventually take over from him.

Carole and Mike now had three children. They were back living in Skelmersdale after living in Liverpool for several years. Mike's initial work placement with James Booth Aluminium had not lived up to the promises it made to its employees. They'd found it hard to manage on his income, so Mike found alternative employment in Imperial Metals in Kirkby. He'd now been there several years and was a foreman in charge of a section. After a difficult start to their marriage, they were getting along comfortably now.

It was now 1977 and unemployment figures were high all over the country. The government had brought in a new 'Early Retirement Scheme', which meant if you retired one year earlier than you were supposed to, they would pay you an income for that year. This, of course, freed up some jobs for the young school leavers who were having problems finding employment.

I thought it was an excellent opportunity for me to finish work. I had, after all, been working throughout my life. This entitled me to my own government pension in my own name, regardless of George's contributions.

Carole had been allocated a really nice council house when she returned to Skelmersdale for the second time. It backed onto woodland and had been built for private sale, but the building firm had gone bankrupt, and the council had bought them out taking over the whole estate. These houses, unlike the typical new town houses, had front and back gardens and proper roads and streets. Carole moved there in June 1976, that gloriously hot summer. This part of Skelmersdale was still being built and there were some beautiful pensioners' flats just being started. At Carole's suggestion, George and I put our names down for one. We thought that while we were waiting to be allocated a property, this would be the perfect time for us to finally visit our son and his family in Australia.

We gave up our third story flat in Croxteth and moved in with Carole and her three sons for a few months, whilst we continued saving for our Australian trip. We'd informed Skelmersdale council of our intentions and the time we expected to return to England, so we weren't too bothered that we'd be offered a place in our absence. It was a tight squeeze in Carole's house. She had to put her three boys together in one room whilst George and I crammed our double bed and a few other furniture items in the smallest bedroom. We couldn't fully open the door because of the double bed, but we managed quite comfortably. The rest of our furniture was stored with various other relatives who were good enough to offer to take it.

The day of our long overdue trip finally arrived. George and I were both very excited as this was our very first flight, and such a long one with neither of us knowing what to expect. We had no need to worry; everything turned out well. Even so, we were happy to reach Sydney Airport and we were looking forward to seeing our dear son Victor again and meeting all the family, most of them for the first time. Although we both felt fine after the long journey, Robyn our daughter-in-law, made sure we went straight to bed for a much needed rest.

The following day, Victor told us he'd bought a small house in Mayfield, not too far away from his own home in Adamstown—a suburb of Newcastle in New South Wales. He told us he wanted us to make it our home for the six months we were staying in Australia. It was a very nice house. We were very happy there, making new friends of our neighbours as well as the social contact we had with our family.

Our Australian neighbours ended up being very good friends of ours. Joan, who lived next door, was forever pulling our leg about us sleeping in of a morning as they were usually up by six o'clock. Jessie, whose back garden backed onto our back garden, was always giving us samples of her baking and other things. There was something from her every day. We kept in touch with them for years afterwards and always sent cards and presents at Christmas. That first time in Australia I have to say was the best. I used to love doing the washing and all the chores there. We had a lovely back garden growing all kinds of fruit and vegetables too.

During our stay in Australia, we spent three or four weeks on a trip to Melbourne. We have a niece out there, the daughter of my husband's sister Hannah. We spent a week travelling to see her, camping along the way, and another week camping on the way back.

One time when we were putting our small tent up for the night, we saw a group of people over by a peach orchard. George and I walked over to see what the attraction was, and these people were filling their buckets and other containers with these beautiful peaches. We were amazed. George and I joined in and collected some peaches for ourselves. We put them in the boot and the next day, carried on with our journey. Unbeknown to us, we had to cross the border.

When we arrived there, the officer we met came from Scotland. He seemed delighted to be chatting with us, and we talked for ages with him about all sorts of interesting things. We only found out later that we weren't supposed to carry fruit or any vegetation over the borders as it can spread pests from one state to another, and there we were with a car boot full of peaches. We gave them to our niece when we reached her place. We had a lovely time in Melbourne and came back to Mayfield to find the garden really overgrown.

It was now 1978; we'd left England in November 1977. Carole, our daughter, wrote regularly to keep us in touch about the new flats being built in Skelmersdale. In one letter, she told us there was only one block left with the four flats almost completed. She hoped we would soon arrive back to claim one of them before they were allocated to someone else. We did get back in time and were given the first of the four remaining flats in Irwell. We moved into the flat on the 6th July 1978. It was my husband's birthday so I could never forget that.

We moved a lot of our stuff into the flat and didn't want to leave it there with the place unoccupied, so George and I slept on the floor. Even though it was July, it was really cold that night with no carpet on the hard floor and no heating on either. Our bed came the following day. Looking back, I can hardly believe it was so long ago.

We have been very fortunate as things turned out; we've been over to Australia five times in all. We never thought we'd ever get there again after the first time. Our second trip out there was paid for by our two sons, Brian and Victor, for our fiftieth wedding anniversary. Our daughter Carole gave us a lovely party up at Stopforth's Barn, near Ashurst Beacon. All our relatives and friends were there and that's where our sons gave us the tickets for our second trip. That time we stayed for nine months, but the house in Mayfield had been sold, and we stayed in Victor's comfortable caravan which was situated in his garden.

We thought our fourth trip in 1991 was definitely our last, but then Carole, who'd never been, said she was going for Victor's eldest son's wedding. We'd all been sent invitations, but hadn't really thought about going again until Carole said she was going alone, as her husband didn't want to fly. This was her last chance to see her brother's family all together before his children married and left home. We spent that morning on the telephone as we called Brian and Joan to say we couldn't let Carole go on her own, and that we were thinking of going with her. Then Brian and Joan called me back to say they were thinking of going too. In the end, the five of us went to see Shane, our grandson, and his lovely wife, Megan, get married.

It was a lovely wedding, and it was a special time being together again with all three of our children for those three weeks. It was doubly precious in hindsight, for Brian, who'd suffered with Multiple Sclerosis for a number of years, died from Cancer six weeks after we returned from Australia. No-one had even known he had it. The following year, Shane and Megan came over here on a twelve month working holiday and it was lovely to have them to stay, especially as Victor came over for a short stay while they were here. My son, Victor, is a regular visitor now, coming every couple of years.

It's good that he does come, as George and I are getting too old now to be going over there. In fact, we don't get out much now at all. George is now ninety and I'm eighty six. Our marriage, lasting 68 years and still counting, has been a very happy one. We've had our ups and downs like everyone but, as my story shows, we have a strong bond and a loving family, just as I had at the beginning of my story with my lovely parents. You don't get much luckier than that.

POSTSCRIPT

Added by Carole Parkes

It is now 2017. Ten years have passed since my mother added the final paragraphs to her life story. In 2010, my parents, George and Elizabeth (Betty), gave up their Skelmersdale flat and went to live in a care home for their final years. Although we had helped to care for them in their own home for many years, my husband's heart condition meant we couldn't take them in. They celebrated their 75th wedding anniversary at Aaron Crest nursing home with family and staff. Victor came over from Australia for that happy occasion as he has done every year in their latter years of life.

I'm so proud my mother finished her story. It is something to pass on to future generations who I hope will be as happy as she and dad were. I feel blessed to have had such wonderful parents.

I fondly remember the wonderful weekends and summer holidays we spent in our caravan at Talacre, North Wales. How we used to repeatedly climb up the huge sand hills on the beach and roll back down again until we were too exhausted to do it anymore. Then we'd head to the sea for a paddle and maybe build a sandcastle. Thank you so much, mum and dad, for giving us such a blessed childhood.

Even though my parents both worked full time and, by today's standards, left us on our own far too much, I know we children were all loved. We certainly grew up and were street wise far sooner than the children of today.

I even remember when, at the age of twelve, I cycled to the caravan with a school friend. It was thirty miles away from our house, so quite a ride. Reaching the Pier Head, we took the ferry across the River Mersey to Birkenhead, and then cycled the rest of the way to our holiday home. We were only there a couple of hours before we had to come straight back again. I hadn't even asked permission to go, thinking my mum and dad wouldn't even know because they were out working.

My beloved father, George, died in May 2012, aged 97. It was just two weeks before their 76th wedding anniversary. My mother, Betty, died the following November at the age of 94. They are resting in the cemetery at St Michael of all Angels, Dalton in Lancashire. Please feel free to place a few flowers there if you are passing.

ELIZABETH ALKER'S ANCESTRY

(All birth, marriage, and death events took place in Lancashire, England.)

Generation 1 — ELIZABETH ALKER was born 24th Feb 1918 in Pemberton, Wigan. She died 6th Nov 2012 in Aaron Crest Nursing Home, Skelmersdale and was buried in Saint Michael of All Angels, Dalton.

Elizabeth married GEORGE WILLIAM SMIH, son of William Smith and Sarah Agnes Thistlewood, 27th May 1936 in St John's, Pemberton, Wigan. George was born 6th Jul 1914 in West Derby, Liverpool. He died 9th May 2012 in Aaroncrest Care Home, Skelmersdale, and was buried with his wife of 75 years in St Michael of All Angels, Dalton.

***

Generation 2 — Elizabeth's father, JAMES ALKER, was born 1st Jan 1875 in Pemberton, Wigan. He married Ellen Pennington 10th Oct 1917 in St John, Pemberton. He died 22 Feb 1933 and was buried in St John, Pemberton.

Generation 2 — Elizabeth's mother, ELLEN PENNINGTON, was born 10th Jan 1893 in Winstanley. She died 1st Mar 1938 in Billinge Hospital, Orrell. The cause of death was Chronic Nephritis. She was buried in St John, Pemberton, Wigan

***

Generation 3 — Elizabeth's paternal grandfather, WILLIAM ALKER, was born Feb or Mar 1851 in Pemberton, Wigan. He married Jane Edgar 14th Apr

1874 in The Wesleyan Chapel, Wigan, and died 1935 in Winstanley, Wigan.

Generation 3 — Elizabeth's paternal grandmother, JANE EDGAR, was born 3rd Nov 1848 in Newburgh, and baptised 28th Jan 1849 in Douglas Chapel, Parbold. She died 1911 in Mellings Farm, Pemberton, and was buried on 12th Aug 1911 in St John the Devine, Pemberton.

Generation 3 —Elizabeth's maternal grandfather, WILLIAM PENNINGTON, was born 25th Apr 1869 in Billinge. He died 4th Feb 1937 in Pemberton, Wigan, and was buried in St John, Pemberton. He married Elizabeth Barton 17th Sep 1892 in The Parish Church, Pemberton, Wigan.

Generation 3 — Elizabeth's maternal grandmother, ELIZABETH BARTON, was born 25th Aug 1869 in Winstanley. She died Feb 1929 in Pemberton, Wigan, and was buried in St John, Pemberton, Wigan.

**

Generation 4 — Elizabeth's paternal great grandfather, JAMES ALKER, was born in Ince, and baptised 5th Mar 1815 in All Saints, Wigan. He died 1st Mar 1886 in Mellings Farm, Pemberton, and was buried 4th Mar 1886 in St John the Devine, Pemberton. He married Margaret Taberner on 12th Mar 1848 in the Wesleyan Methodist Chapel, Wigan.

Generation 4 — Elizabeth's paternal great grandmother, MARGARET TABERNER, was born 20th May 1811 in Pemberton, Wigan, and baptised 14th Jun 1811 in All Saints, Wigan. She died before 1881.

Generation 4 — Elizabeth's paternal great grandfather is unknown.

Generation 4 — Elizabeth's paternal great grandmother, MARY EDGAR, was born 1828/1829 in Hoscar Moss. She married John Spencer 21st Oct 1865 in St Peter & St Paul, Ormskirk. JOHN SPENCER is not blood related to Elizabeth He was born about 1828 in Newburgh.

Generation 4 — Elizabeth's maternal great grandfather, JOHN PENNINGON, was born 11th Oct 1818 in Rainford. He married Ann Fishwick on 7 Nov 1865 in Wigan.

Generation 4 —Elizabeth's maternal great grandmother ANN FISHWICK, was born 21st Jul 1828 in Billinge, and baptised 27th Jul 1828 in Billinge.

Generation 4 — Elizabeth's maternal great grandfather ISAAC BARTON, was born 22nd May 1847 in Pemberton, Wigan, and died on 2nd Apr 1910 in Manor House Farm, Wigan. He married Ellen Johnson on 8th Aug 1869 in Billinge.

Generation 4 — Elizabeth's maternal great grandmother, ELLEN JOHNSON, was born 1841/1843 in Knotty Ash, West Derby.

REFERENCES

[i] Pemberton, formerly a township in Wigan ecclesiastical parish, became part of the County Borough of Wigan, Lancashire, England, in 1904.

[ii] My mother's uncle, Isaac BARTON, was born 12th March 1880 Pemberton, Lancashire, England, and died 1970. He and his wife, Martha BUTTERWORTH, born 1874 Poynton, Cheshire, had two sons and three daughters. Their children were: William BARTON 1903, Ellen 1905, Margaret 1906, Hannah 1908, and Isaac 1911.

One of this Isaac Barton's uncles and a few of his cousins emigrated to Utah, USA around 1862 and became well regarded Mormons. This uncle was John BARTON 1806 – 1874, High Priest, and his cousins were; William Bell BARTON 1836 – 1923, High Priest; Isaac 1842 – 1916, Bishop of 19th Ward; and Joseph 1848 – 1932, President of the 143d quorum seventies and 34 quorum elders of Davis stake. They are featured in the book 'Pioneers and Prominent Men of Utah'.

[iii] My father, James ALKER, born 1875 in Pemberton and died 1933 Pemberton, was the son of William ALKER 1851 – 1935 and Jane Edgar 1848 – 1911 of Mellings Farm, Winstanley, Lancashire. Mellings farm no longer exists as a farm. A housing estate called Mellings Farm now occupies the land. My father was a gentle, loving man who comes from a long line of Lancashire farmers.

His two older siblings, James William Edgar ALKER, born 1870, and Arthur ALKER 1873 – 1955, were illegitimate. Both of these brothers were baptised with the surname EDGAR, but later became known by the surname ALKER. James' younger siblings were: Margaret Ann born 1876/1877, who married James TURNER and farmed Windy Arbour Farm; Samuel 1877/1878 – 1950, who died in Buenos Aries, Argentina; Elizabeth 1880 – 1969, a spinster; Alfred 1881/1882 – 1941, who died Dyserth, Flintshire, Wales; Herbert 1884/1885 – 1931; Thomas 1890; and Stanley 1892/1893 – 1950.

[iv] John Ackers ALKER born around 1871 was my father's cousin. He was the son of Samuel ALKER 1848 – 1915, born Pemberton, and the grandson of James ALKER 1815 – 1886, who died at Mellings Farm, Winstanley. John Ackers ALKER farmed Chapel House Farm, Pemberton. His wife, Catharine PHYTHIAN died there.

[v] My maternal grandfather, William PENNINGTON 1869 – 1937, was born in Billinge. He was the son of John PENNINGTON, a gamekeeper born 1818 in Rainford, and Ann FISHWICK, born 1828 in Billinge. The parents of John 1818 were William PENNINGTON 1891, and Jane BIRCH 1788, both born in Rainford, Lancashire.

[vi] My maternal grandmother, Elizabeth PENNINGTON (nee BARTON), was born 25th August 1969 in The Arches, Winstanley. She was the daughter of Isaac BARTON 1847 – 1910, born in Pemberton, and Ellen JOHNSON 1841 – 1843, born in Knotty Ash,

West Derby, Liverpool. Their other children were Mary BARTON 1871, Ellen 1873, William 1874, Ann 1875, Alice 1876, Nancy 1877, Isaac 1880, and Jane 1881.

[vii] My mother's siblings were: Ann PENNINGTON 1894 – 1968, John 1900, Margaret 1901, William 1903, Jane 1906, Nancy 1908, and Alice 1910.

[viii] My father-in-law, William SMITH, was born 10th November 1888 in Liverpool. He was the son of George Henry SMITH 1857 – 1903, plumber and gas fitter of Liverpool, and Mary Jane HOLT 1865 – 1946. Mary Jane's grandfather was Joseph Holt born about 1796 in Ireland. We believe he may be related to General Joseph Holt of the 1798 Irish rebellion. The naming pattern of his, and his only son's children, suggests Joseph could be descended from one of General Holt's brothers. This has yet to be proven.

[ix] Late 16th Century house in Winstanley, built for the Winstanley family in the 1560's. They were Lords of the manor as early as 1252. I have an account written in the 1920's by Samuel FOURACRE of Rylance Farm, Winstanley. In this, he names all the workers at Winstanley Hall, and lists Margaret as Maggie PENNINGTON, working in the gardens.

[x] Mary Jane SMITH (nee HOLT) 1865 – 1946, daughter of Thomas Joshua HOLT 1834 – 1895 and Ann BOOTH 1836/1837 – 1928, was born in Liverpool. There is a distinct possibility she could be related to General Joseph HOLT, protestant leader in the 1798 Irish rebellion. He was exiled to Australia but went with his family as a free man rather than a

prisoner. Perhaps she is a granddaughter of one of his brothers.

[xi] My father-in-law's sister, Rose Lily REDDINGTON (nee SMITH) 1903 – 1980, was born in Liverpool. Her other siblings were: George Henry SMITH born 1885, Ann Hannah 1890/1891, Mary Florence 1893, May 1897, and Thomas Alfred 1890. Rose Lily married Edward Reddington, born 1893 Scotland, in 1934.

[xii] Woodbine Grove, where we lived, was off York Street, which, in turn, was off West Derby Road, a main artery road leading into the town centre. Heading away from the city centre we would go down West Derby Road, through Tuebrook, until we came to the Carlton cinema. There we would turn right along Green Lane and follow it to the end where there were bus sheds. From her we would turn left along a main road, cross it, and then take a short cut through an alleyway between some shops. St Oswald's Gardens, Old Swan, where Aunty Lily lived, was just a couple of streets away from here. I would estimate the whole journey to be a little above two miles.

[xiii] This was the Imperial Chemical Industries.

[xiv] My grandfather was William ALKER 1851 – 1935 who farmed Mellings Farm, Winstanley. William married Jane EDGAR in 1874. She was illegitimate, born 1848 in Lathom, and died 1911 at Mellings Farm. Their children were: James William Edgar ALKER, an illegitimate son born 1870; Arthur ALKER 1873 – 1955, also illegitimate; James, 1875 – 1933, my father,

the first legitimate child; Margaret Ann born 1876/1877; Samuel 1877/1878 – 1950, who died in Buenos Aries, Argentina; Elizabeth 1880 – 1969, a spinster; Alfred 1881/1882 – 1941, who died Dyserth, Flintshire, Wales; Herbert 1884/1885 – 1931; Thomas 1890; and Stanley 1892/1893 – 1950. The first two illegitimate sons were baptised with the surname EDGAR. No father's name was present on the record. Surprisingly, Arthur, the second illegitimate son born in 1873, was baptised in 1876, two years after Jane's 1874 marriage to William ALKER, yet he was still baptised as Arthur EDGAR. Both illegitimate children were recorded in census data with the surname ALKER.

My grandfather, William, was the son of James ALKER 1815 – 1886, a farmer of Sledbrook Farm, Pemberton, and Margaret KILSHAW, nee TABERNER, a widow with six children. She was born 1811 in Pemberton.

^{xv} My great grandfather, James ALKER 1815 – 1886, was a farmer in Ince. He later moved to Sledbrook Farm in Pemberton and died there in 1886. This was sometimes called Slaidbrook Farm in the records. This farm was halfway down Enfield Street, Pemberton, between the house numbers 86 and 91 according to the 1881 census. By 1851, James had married Margaret KILSHAW (nee TABERNER), a widow with six children aged from four to sixteen. Her name is sometimes recorded as CULSHAW on some records Margaret had three more children from her marriage to my grandfather: Samuel ALKER 1848 – 1915, who farmed Holmes House Farm; my

grandfather, William 1851; and Elizabeth 1854/1855 – 1879. There were four servants at Sledbrook in the 1861 census, but only two by 1881.

James was the son of my 2x great grandfather, Samuel ALKER 1783 – 1863 and Ann HALLIWELL 1793 – 1856. Samuel first farmed in Ince, and this was where several of his children were born: James 1815, William 1816, Jane 1816, Ellen 1818, and Thomas 1824. By 1826, he was farming Meddow's Farm (sic), near to Bottling wood, Haigh. This was where his daughter Ann was born in 1826. In 1828 and 1831, two more children were born in Pemberton. This may have been at Sledbrook Farm.

^{xvi} My paternal grandmother, Jane EDGAR, was born 3rd November 1848 in 98 Stopforths, Newburgh, next to The Eagle and Child inn. She was baptised 28th January 1849 in St Douglas Chapel, Parbold, and was recorded as the daughter of Mary EDGAR who was born 1828/1829 Hoscar Moss. I know little of Jane except she was the mother of two illegitimate children when she married my grandfather, William ALKER and they went on to have another eight legitimate children. Jane may also have been illegitimate. Although the 1851 census states her mother, Mary, is married, there's no trace of a husband. Mary was the daughter of Thomas EDGAR born 1805/1806 in Eccleston and Elizabeth RAWSTHORNE. This could be the Elizabeth RAWSTHORNE baptised 3rd April 1803 in Ormskirk, but not yet proven.

Jane's mother, my great grandmother, Mary EDGAR married John SPENCER 21st October 1965 in

Ormskirk, and she had two further children: Alfred SPENCER baptised 14th February 1869 in Skelmersdale, and Richard SPENCER born about 1871 in Skelmersdale. She already had Jane EDGAR, my grandmother, and her son, John EDGAR born 20th January 1852 in Newburgh and baptised 21st March 1852 Parbold.

[xvii] John Ackers ALKER, born about 1871 in Pemberton, was the son of Samuel ALKER 1848 – 1915 and Jane A ACKERS born 1849. John married Catharine PHYTHIAN 1867 – 1946 in 1903, and they farmed Chapel Street Farm in Pemberton.

[xviii] James TURNER born about 1877, farmer of Windy Arbour Farm, Winstanley, was the son of John TURNER born 1841 Upholland, and Ellen born 1841 Langho.

[xix] Alfred ALKER, a carpenter, was born 1881/1882 in Mellings Farm and died 29th January at The Red Lion Hotel, Dyserth, Flintshire, Wales. His address at the time of his death was Woodbury Rose Hill, St Asaph. He was buried at St Asaph. It is believed Alfred and his wife Emily Foster had no issue because he left £200 to each of his nieces.

[xx] Impington Hall, a large mansion built for the Pepys family was sold to the Chivers Company in 1921. They had no intention of living in it, but hoped it could be used for educational and community purposes. Indeed, they provided free educational classes there for their own workforce for some time. The hall was later gifted to the Cambridgeshire Education Committee.

The army was billeted there during WW2 and later the hall fell into disrepair. It no longer exists.

^{xxi} My mother-in-law, Sarah Agnes THISTLEWOOD was born 21st February 1890 in Liverpool and died 1967 in Douglas Bank nursing home, Appley Bridge. She was the daughter of George THISTLEWOOD 1851 – 1929 and Sarah Annie EVANS 1851 – 1899. They were both born in Liverpool. George was a lithographic printer and bell ringer. Sarah Agnes's grandfather and previous Thistlewood ancestors were prominent captains in bell ringing circles.

^{xxii} Many families had lost everything in the bombing raids, their homes, furniture, clothes, and bedding. In the aftermath of war, these things were not easy to replace. Often, the men who did return were not capable of working, at least, not right away. Such deprived families used orange boxes and the like as substitute chairs, tables, and dressers.

^{xxiii} My uncle, Samuel ALKER, born about 1878, died 1850. He worked at La Forestal, Guillamina, Santé Fe, Buenos Aries, Argentina, as a bio chemist, and died in the Muniz Hospital, Uspallata, 2272 Buenos Aries. His estate totalled £14,258 6s 5d which solicitors Randolph Hatton Gee and Richard Stanley Gee dealt with.

A copy of his will states all his assets are to be converted to gilt edged shares, and his sister, Elizabeth ALKER is to receive an allowance for life from their income. On her death, nineteen years later, the shares were sold and the estate divided into seven shares to be distributed to his six nieces and nephews. I received two shares. I believe my Uncle Sam bequeathed it this way because I was an orphan with no siblings.

My Uncle Sam gained a B.Sc.Hon degree in Lancaster. He was a student of agriculture in the 1901 census, living at 7 Frenchwood Street, the home of William MOLYNEUX, a cotton cloth looker from Hindley. Another fellow student living there was James BROWN from Prestwick, Westmoreland.